# YOU

## and Everything Else

### MANAGING CONTEXTICA: YOUR PLACES AND TIMES

by

Richard F. Manning

AHA PUBLISHING COMPANY

ISBN 09723663-O-X

First printing September 2002

AHA PUBLISHING COMPANY
1041 Forest Lakes Drive
Naples, FL 34105

## Disclaimer (the fine print)

The purpose of this book is to inform, educate and entertain in the pursuit of its goals: developing an appreciation of the tremendous importance of the contexts we choose, and, enhancing creative thinking skills in helping to select the most fortuitous time and place circumstances in the many areas of our lives. In doing so, the author ventures into many domains such as: parenting, education, occupations, relationships, retirement, sex, finance, medicine, drugs, etc.

The publisher and author are not engaged in rendering legal, medical or other professional services. If such assistance is required, the services of a competent professional should be sought. This text should only be used as a general guide subject to the reader's personal evaluation.

Thus, the author and Aha Publishing Company shall have neither liability nor responsibility to any person or entity with respect to any loss or damage caused, or alleged to be caused, directly or indirectly by the information contained in this book.

# CONTENTS

*Introduction* *i*

*Chapter One* ***People, Places and Times*** ........ *1*

*Chapter Two* ***Good Contexters, Bad Contexters*** ........ *13*

*Chapter Three* ***Creative Thinking, Part One*** ........ *20*

*Chapter Four* ***Creative Thinking, Part Two*** ........ *34*

*Chapter Five* ***Four Steps to Creatively Contexting Your Life*** ........ *59*

*Chapter Six* ***Contextica: Early Years, Schooling and Work*** ........ *79*

*Chapter Seven* ***Contextica: Relationships*** ........ 100

*Chapter Eight* ***Time Really Is of the Essence*** ........ *129*

*Chapter Nine* ***The Contextica of Money*** ........ *146*

*Chapter Ten* ***Putting It All in the Proper Context*** ........ *167*

*References* *201*

# INTRODUCTION

When was the last time you made a really good move? And when was the last time you did something that you wished you hadn't? We're all human, thus all of us have made good and bad decisions which have affected our lives positively or negatively. So it should go without saying (but I'm going to say it anyway) that we should, of course, strive to make smart choices and avoid making not-very-prudent ones. It's not easy. This book offers a unique perspective to help you do just that.

Consider:

- A morning jogger along La Brea Boulevard in Los Angeles may be racing to a premature death.
- A television producer uses all her influence to get a new sitcom pilot into the Thursday, 8:00 P.M. time slot.
- An attorney argues strenuously for a change of venue and a trial date postponement for his client.

Each of the three exemplifies the critical importance of the place and time contexts of our lives. Running during rush-hour traffic in the trail of deadly carbon monoxide fumes is patently stupid. Television programs aired in certain spots and times are virtually assured a large audience. The lawyer knows there will be a much better chance of winning if the case can go before jurors who are away from local publicity and if there is more time for people to forget. Two instances of good contexting, one of bad.

Your life can be looked at as comprising (1) ***you***, the individual, and (2) ***everything else*** around you: the clothes you wear, your home, school, workplace, the air you breathe, your husband, wife, relatives, friends, your car, community, country, planet, earth and beyond . . . literally all of the other physical things in your environment. Life, then, may be simply defined as you interacting with your surroundings. But that wouldn't be accurate. No, the two interact in that mysterious dimension called (3) ***time***. The latter two — our physical environment and time — comprise our ***contextica***.

Happiness, fulfillment and satisfaction in life are directly related to our circumstances, spatial and temporal . . . being in the right places at the right times. This book has two purposes: to emphasize the tremendous importance these spatio-temporal contexts have on our lives, and to provide the reader with proven techniques for creatively choosing the best contextica — the right places and the right times. The premise is that many of us tend to continue in situations which are not satisfying or desirable, yet we remain in them though there are boundless options in our free society. Indeed, many live their lives in a state of Thoreau's "quiet desperation," muddling through this journey without ever achieving God-given potentials. My mission is to help you develop a keen awareness and appreciation of your contextica.

The word "context" is usually used in our lexicon as in "he took my words out of context." The point being that a different or incorrect interpretation is made as opposed to what was intended. My usage refers to it as it relates to space and time. But it became awkward to differentiate between a context of space and of time so I've concocted the word "contextica" to cover both. There is also no such word as "contexting" (until now), so I took the liberty of creating that verb form of the noun following the suit of those who made "impacting" from "impact."

There are some cliches scattered throughout the text for which I make no apologies as they impart some pretty good wisdom. When people disparage a cliche with a disdainful "that's a cliche" . . . aren't they themselves guilty of using a cliche?

The examples given of people making good or bad choices of contextica are from true life experiences. Where there could be a possibility of embarrassment, I've changed the names to avoid any such indignity (and also, frankly, to protect my derriere).

Although there are chapters on relationships and finances, I certainly would not profess to be an expert in those areas. There are tons of really good books (some listed in the reference section) about improving your love life or making a fortune in the stock market. My *sole* aim in venturing into those areas is to show the relation to creative contexting. So be forewarned. The suggestions made in those chapters should be taken with your own subjective grain of salt.

As to the rest of the material, it is the result of a lifetime of passionate interest in the field of creative thinking and is based on solid research, personal and professional experience, and much that you will recognize as just good old common sense. This book is only an introduction to the fantastic possibilities of applying creative thinking to your unique contextica. Please read further in this exciting area.

Everyone wants to be happy and successful, achieve financial security, accomplish something meaningful and relate well to those around us. In these pages you will be offered a different and unique perspective for accomplishing all that. I sincerely hope you find them informative, occasionally funny, challenging and — *most of all* — ***useful***.

## Chapter One

# PEOPLE, PLACES AND TIMES

**"Man is not the creature of circumstances,<br>circumstances are the creature of man."<br>— Disraeli**

With all due respect, Ben, I strongly disagree with you. Men and women are definitely shaped by their circumstances and are, to a very large extent, the products of their environments. That is the central theme of this book. We can choose from different settings or create new conditions to better suit our lives, but once in those contexts, we will — for better or worse — be absolutely affected. Most of us don't fully appreciate the tremendous influence our personal, social, geographic, and temporal contexts have on us. Disraeli errs big time in ignoring the importance of our contexts. Of approximately six billion earthlings, who are about the same biologically, each of us is different because of *where* we are and *when* we are living. The two together constitute our CONTEXTICA.

## We Are All Chameleons

That amazing lizard (Chamaeleontidae) becomes green if reposing on a green setting or brown when languishing on a brown context in order to escape its many hungry predators. That quick-change artist is certainly the master of camouflage. Soldiers have long tried to emulate by wearing earth-tone color uniforms. While we humans certainly don't change colors quite so dramatically, we do respond to our physical contexts almost as amazingly as the versatile chameleon. That first careless sunning on the beach will change a pale skin to a painful lobster red in minutes . . . a defense mechanism in action. In heat, we'll also perspire to lessen body temperature. If in a cold setting, we'll shiver to increase body warmth. When a surgeon's scalpel makes an incision into a patient's anesthetized body, blood pressure and pulse will immediately spike up as an automatic defense against the invader. When you walk into a room full of people, your blood pressure will rise. As you leave the room alone, your pressure will lower. That wonderful propensity of the body to maintain itself (homeostasis) enables us to be creatures in almost any circumstance. We can — with suitable accommodations like clothing, oxygen masks, scuba gear — live virtually anywhere. We can stay for years in the ocean's depths in nuclear-powered submarines and survive indefinitely in outer space stations.

Ever been in a group when someone starts yawning and you also start yawning? Same phenomenon with itching and scratching. We respond to our social contexts very consistently. If you're with a group of laughing people, you'll probably also laugh . . . or at least smile.

That's why those clever comedy sitcom producers go to great lengths to build canned laughter in their programs. They full well know that mirth is contagious.

When among the silent, as on an elevator, you'll conform to the silence. Otherwise sane, rational people will yell at the very tops of their lungs at a football game . . . painting their faces, rising and sitting for "the wave" and becoming part of the madding crowd. When in Rome, we do indeed become Romans!

**When in Rome, we do, indeed, become Romans.**

We cannot help but conform to our contexts. We ***are*** our contexts. They shape and alter our lives every minute of every day of every year. We need to better understand and more fully appreciate these powerful influences and realize that we have the power to change them as it befits us. It is also our extremely good fortune to be living in a society which allows and even facilitates change. In most other countries, contexts are predetermined. Democracies provide for freedom of choice and freedom of movement — a most wonderful and glorious situation.

### *Only in America*

By the grace of "whatever Gods may be," we live in the best of all contexts — these blessed United States of America. We Americans have more money, cars, homes, TVs, computers, hospitals, schools and colleges per capita than just about any other country. But most important, we have freedom — which is so easy to take for granted.

When I was a pupil in a Chicago elementary school, the entire student body sang the national anthem and pledged allegiance to the flag every morning. We were regularly taught about our country's proud ideals of liberty, justice, equality, and brotherhood "from sea to shining sea." As a child, however, the concepts never really took hold. Sort of like a mother's constant admonitions to her children. They know she means well, but after a while she gets tuned out. So it was that the singing and the pledge became rote, meaningless exercises. High school literature teachers have long lamented that trying to impart Shakespeare to teenagers is futile, for most will not understand or appreciate the Bard until adulthood. It took a TV repairman and a Cuban refugee to make me realize how lucky I was to have been born in the good old U.S. of A.

Some years ago I had to call for service on a balky TV set. When the technician finished, the set worked better than ever. Impressed with his work and the very reasonable bill, I offered him some coffee and inquired about his background which, judging from his accent, had to be European. He told me he was from Czechoslovakia where he was an electrical engineer before emigrating here three years ago. I asked why he would forsake a professional position in the country of his birth to come here and his answer was both brief and emphatic.

"Freedom!"

But he was working long hours at a level below his educational status. How was he more free?

**"Don't you know everyone wants to come to your wonderful country?"**

He looked at me incredulously. In his communist land, he explained, he could never do what he was doing here — going where he pleased, opening his own business and reaping the rewards of his labor. In Czechoslovakia, he went on, the government decides how and where one functions. He then said, "Don't you know everyone wants to come to your wonderful country?" He really told me nothing I didn't already know, but hearing it from a non-American gave me a new and deeper appreciation of being a nephew of Uncle Sam.

Several years later, another immigrant — a young Cuban woman — reinforced that appreciation. She was a "Marielita," one of thousands who fled from Castro's communism in 1980. With her four-year-old son, she boarded an overloaded boat and departed the port of Mariel for the 90-mile journey to Key West, Florida. Seas were choppy and just a few miles out the beleaguered vessel took on water and had to return to Cuba. Some of the terrified passengers reluctantly elected to stay in Cuba rather than again risk drowning in the shark-infested sea, but most — the young woman and her son included — boarded the next available craft. They made it to Key West, then to the Krome Avenue Detention Center where they were processed and placed with relatives in Miami. There she learned the language, enrolled in school and became a Registered Nurse. It was in the hospital where she worked that I met her while visiting a sick friend.

In our conversations, I asked what she liked best about being in the United States. She unhesitatingly replied: "Freedom." She related stories of Gestapo-like government control in her native land where there were severe restrictions on travel and state censorship of television, newspapers and books. We Americans easily take the freedoms we have in those areas for granted.

This book about choices of contexts would be meaningless in those two countries. Czechoslovakia has since thrown off its communist shackles while Cuba's rigid system still exists. How fortunate for us that we live in a society of freedom to choose. How sad that so many of us do not make better and fuller use of our options. Why is this so?

Perhaps our contexts are really not that important. Maybe we are who we are because of our genetic inheritance, or luck, or fate. "The die is cast" sort of philosophy then makes this book worthless. Close it immediately and go on to something else. No, just kidding! The point is worthy of consideration, however, and if you stay in your present contextica (reading this book at this time) we'll go to a discussion of one of humankind's most perplexing and fascinating issues.

### *Nature vs. Nurture*

After graduation from a liberal arts university, I was pretty much convinced that human behavior was 90% influenced by the environment and about 10% from heredity. I remember being greatly impressed with B.F. Skinner's *Walden II* in which a totally controlled, scientifically planned community was a Utopia for its inhabitants. Communism (*Walden II* writ large ) is struggling for survival as we begin the twenty-first century. Rigid control, necessary in a socialistic system, narrowed or eliminated the economic, social, geographic and political options of its people. Highly talented Cuban athletes defect to the United States where they can make millions of dollars instead of handfuls of pesos. The need for a large latitude of freedom seems to be inherent in our nature. Strict limitations of contextual choices have proved so unworkable that remaining communist countries are experimenting with varying degrees of capitalism in which more options are available. Does the decline of communism mean the 90% nurture and 10% nature proportion should be reversed?

The controversy as to the relative part each plays in our behavior has puzzled Psych. 101 students for decades. Recently scientists have been discussing it again in attempting to know more about the killers in the Littleton, Colorado school tragedy. Were the young men born with a "bad seed" or was their environment (upbringing, movies, video games, violent culture, etc.) to blame? Society has also been concerned about the causation of homosexuality. Is homosexuality learned or inherited? The answer is not one of simply academic interest but has broad implications for attitudes, funding for AIDS research, legislation for same sex marriages, etc.

There does seem to be an emerging consensus on accepting a 50-50 position. One is certainly born with a range of genetic characteristics which will be enhanced or ignored in a lifetime of various environments. Accepting that there may be a gene or genes for gayness, a person so born may or may not become an active homosexual because of his or her unique environmental interaction with that hereditary factor. Conversely, someone without the genetic predisposition would probably never become gay no matter how favorable the settings. Putting it another way: if a man's genes decreed a height of 5'2", he's never "gonna play in the NBA." Score big for nature.

Nurturists, however, can get a big boost from a 1998 study at Washington University in St. Louis. Scientists there found that a group of Anolis lizards had developed shorter limbs *within only a ten-year period* of having been moved from one island to another. On their second island the vegetation was such that they didn't need longer limbs to reach it. Apparently the rather dramatic morphological change was a quick evolutionary response to their new context. We also know that birds who migrate to areas where there are no predators lose their ability to fly and that goldfish stay small in a bowl but grow large when released to a pond.

That the two, nature and nurture, are *equally* important may or may not be valid. We can be on pretty solid ground, however, if we acknowledge that the interplay of both determines who we are. A tiger can change his habits but not his stripes. Inheritance may bestow a bad heart, but the right physical conditioning and medical care can mitigate the condition. In life as in blackjack, you don't need to have "21" to be a winner. Sometimes a weak hand played smartly is plenty. Our concern here is that our nurture (context) is of tremendous importance but is too often regarded as immutable. We don't fully appreciate how important our contexts are in determining our happiness or lack of it, our successes or failures. Just as we need periodic medical checkups, it is also very important to have regular contextual evaluations.

### *Location, Location, Location . . . Context, Context, Context*

The real estate agent's classic answer to the question of what are the three most important factors in selling a house: "location, location, location." Homes in Naples, Florida, on the seashore sell for a million bucks and up . . . and a very high "up." Just a block away, you can get an equal or better place for half of the prices of those on the beach. Values are directly proportional to the distance from the beach. A well-constructed, beautiful home which is next to an incinerator plant or in the glide path of an airport will certainly be worth much less than an identical house located elsewhere. In life as in real estate, location *is* paramount.

The value of real estate is also closely related to the context of time. During a period of high interest rates, homes will be harder to sell with a consequent lowering of prices. Any real estate agent will tell you that the worst time to sell is in December while the best months are in the spring. Financial gains or losses in buying or selling our homes are definitely determined by these spatio-temporal contexts. The quality of our lives is also directly and absolutely related to where we position ourselves and to timing. We are inescapably shaped by our *contextica* (our places and times). While we would not knowingly buy a house in a poor or unsafe condition, we may unwittingly find ourselves staying in environments which do not foster our best development or help us achieve fuller, more satisfying lives. Worse . . . we may be in harmful or dangerous contexts. Joggers — whose laudable goal is the pursuit of health — are really jeopardizing their well being when they choose to run during rush hours along busy thoroughfares with hundreds of cars spewing carbon monoxide and other noxious chemicals . . . bad timing and placement.

### *The Time of Our Lives*

A friend of mine decided to make a career change and go into real estate sales. He completed the courses, passed the exams, and signed on with one of the biggest firms in the rapidly growing market of Boca Raton, Florida. He traded in his convertible for the required luxury sedan to impress his clients. He made the right contextual choices, except for one, and didn't make a dime of commissions after a year of energetic effort! The one wrong contextual factor? The year was 1981 . . . the time of abnormally high interest rates for mortgages. He *was* in the right place but at the *wrong* time. Disgusted, he took a job as a security guard for a few years and then in 1996 returned to real estate after interest rates had gone to much lower levels. A member of the "million dollar club" and a consistent "salesperson of the month," he now enjoys a very high income because today he is in the right place *and* at the right time.

The lawyer's adage, "time is of the essence," is certainly appropriate. While we cannot manage time ("time management" is a misnomer, we can only manage ourselves in relation to time), we can give more attention to selecting the best time contexts so as to avoid the Realtor's hapless experience. We won't be concerned here with those methods of managing time better: keeping a log, prioritizing tasks, handling papers once, use of the telephone, etc. Our emphasis in a later chapter will be on selecting the best time contexts. Since "time's a-flyin'," let's go on to:

### *From Caves to Space Bases*

We are genetically engineered to be constantly expanding our contexts. Humankind's primitive ancestors left their caves as families and combined into tribes who formed villages, then cities, then kingdoms, and finally nations. The Polynesians braved thousands of miles of open seas in fragile crafts to seek new lands. Asians probably walked across the Aleutian Islands area to Alaska. The English, Dutch, Portuguese, Spanish, and French sent their ships to every part of the world. It is apparent . . . we were not designed to stay in one place.

We have, indeed, the ability to choose from many contexts. I can leave my Florida home after breakfast and fly over to Germany for supper. One of my sons is a writer-producer in Los Angeles and the other is a cable sales executive in Minneapolis. One daughter-in-law is working in Japan. Her mother is in Uruguay. Much of this book was written on cruise ships plying the Caribbean — my context of choice for that activity. Truly, we can live, work or play wherever we choose. And now, we are well underway to moving towards our next great expansion — that "final (?) frontier"

— space. Walking on the moon, taking pictures of the surface of Mars, erecting space stations are all realities . . . no longer regarded as dreams but as the expected progression of our technological genius. No doubt, a few generations from now these great achievements will be viewed as elementary beginnings, much like Columbus's first forays to the new world. By the end of 1997, Austrian researchers succeeded in destroying bits of light in one place and making exact replicas appear three feet away! Scientisits in Australia duplicated that feat in 2002. Is this the beginning of a "beam me up Scotty" technology? Space seems certainly to be our next evolutionary context.

### *Mirror, Mirror on the Wall*

Walk up to the next person you see with a great big smile on your face. You can safely bet that he or she will also smile. Frown at someone and you'll likely get a frown in return. We and our contexts interact . . . each affects the other. The countenance you present will be reflected by the other person. A haughty sales clerk is short with you and you react in kind. We mirror those around us as well as we mirror the weather. A bright, mild sunny day makes us feel happy and alive. A grey, rainy day dampens our spirits.

To be redundantly redundant (?): we *are* to a very great extent — much more than most of us realize most of the time — directly affected by our times and surroundings. Regularly evaluating our contexts can be an invaluable habit in enhancing our lives. A periodic introspection can lead us to make major or minor changes. At the least, if no changes seem warranted, we can then feel satisfied that we're doing O.K., that we're not like corks floating in an ocean going wherever the waves or currents dictate. We are, rather, captains of our own ships determining for ourselves what waters we will sail and which direction we will chart. Eschewing being on automatic pilot, we can fly to wherever we please. Now, more than ever, we have the opportunity to lead richer, fuller, more productive lives. Blessed with independence in this great country of ours, we have the freedom and flexibility to change. Creatively contexting our lives ensures that we can be the "creatures" who are the beneficiaries of our own deliberately-selected circumstances. Benjamin Disraeli was just half right.

**We have the opportunity to lead richer, fuller, more productive lives.**

## Chapter Two

# GOOD CONTEXTERS — BAD CONTEXTERS

**"He that walketh with wise men shall be wise, but**
**a companion of fools shall be destroyed."**
**Proverbs 14:7**

Well, "destroyed " may be too harsh; let's just change that to "a fool also." Since we've had the temerity to challenge Disraeli, a little revision of this Biblical wisdom isn't too much a leap. The proverb does support this book's contention that our contexts have a tremendous, but many times unappreciated, influence on what we become. Nike ran a successful television advertising campaign some years ago which trumpeted that "image is everything." Nonsense . . . *Context is everything.*

Our images are simply the results or reflections of our contextual choices as we'll see in looking at six people whose lives were changed dramatically by their times and surroundings.

### *Surgeon, Submariner, and Scribe*

If you've enjoyed the movie *Coma* or read any of his more than twenty medical thrillers, you'll know the name Robin Cook. Many of his books have been made into motion pictures and, fortunately for us, more are in the making. He created a whole new genre of medical mysteries which not only entertain but challenge our thinking as well. Dr. Cook, an ophthalmologist, lends just enough credence to his plots to make them plausible.

What you may not know is that his writing career began during his stint as an officer aboard a U.S. Navy nuclear submarine. During the long and somewhat monotonous undersea cruises, tending to the health needs of the crew and his other duties were not enough to keep boredom at bay. Dr. Cook's fertile imagination found an outlet in his decision to put his confining context to good use.

**Creative contexter extraordinaire!**

He took advantage of his isolation to begin a second career as a writer. No phone calls, no television, no knocks on the door from would-be tennis or golf partners, no shopping, no immediate mail to answer . . . a very minimum of distractions. This spatio-temporal context was the birthplace of his many fascinating and spellbinding medical mysteries which have placed his name among the literary giants of our time. Dr. Robin Cook — creative contexter extraordinaire!

### *Talk Show Icon*

Phil Donahue is generally acknowledged as the father of present-day talk show hosts. He is also an outstanding example of the masterful use of context. His show originated in Dayton, Ohio. After its resounding success there, he moved it to Chicago, a central location which provided access to larger audiences and celebrity guests. After several years in the Windy City, the views of the Merchandise Mart and the Lake Michigan skyline in the opening credits were replaced by vistas of the Statue of Liberty and Manhattan skyscrapers. Donahue recognized the importance of changing contexts in order to keep the show fresh and vibrant.

Another factor which contributed to the longstanding success of his show was his contextual savvy in hosting it. Moving about the audience with a cordless microphone, he was like a symphony orchestra conductor wielding his baton to increase or decrease the volume or pace of the music. Donahue extended the microphone/baton to members of the audience, quickly retrieving it if the comments were off base, or staying with the participant who was worthy of more time. But, unlike the orchestra conductor who weaves his magic from a raised podium in front of his musicians, Donahue aligned himself for most of his programs *with* the audience, moving through it from person to person thus allying himself with his public and dissociating the host from his often-controversial podium guests. This moving about in his context assured his viewers that he was neutral, interested in bringing out all sides of the topic. Another very good creative contexter.

### *A Mother's Dream*

Mitzi Ross, a bright, vivacious girl, worked in the family tailor shop in Cleveland, Ohio. At twenty-two, Mitzi had been "always the bridesmaid, never the bride" for almost all of her high school friends. She longed to meet and marry a nice guy — preferably a doctor or other professional — and raise a family.

Although many twenty-two-year-old women give considerable thought to those goals, few set out to reach them as directly and aggressively as did Mitzi. She simply decided to place herself in contexts in which she would have a greater chance of meeting with suitable candidates. The tailor shop was about three miles from Case Western Reserve University, where hundreds of young men study for careers in medicine, law, engineering and other professions. Every day for her lunch hour during favorable weather, Mitzi boarded a Euclid Avenue bus for the ten-minute ride to the campus. There on the steps of either the law library or the medical library, she would eat her lunch. Scores (no pun intended) of single students similarly inclined were her companions. After over thirty such journeys, as you may have guessed by now, she met a medical student, fell in love, became the bride instead of the bridesmaid and is now living happily with her gynecologist husband and two children in Shaker Heights, Ohio. A perfect case of creative contexting: Mitzi had decided what she wanted of life, put herself in a contextica most likely to achieve that goal, and then had the chutzpah and perseverance to carry out her plan.

### *Two Presidents Who Never Were*

**"Of all sad words of tongue and pen — the saddest, 'it might have been.' "**
**— Thomas Paine**

The surgeon-writer, former talk show host, and the single woman are outstanding examples of smart use of contexts. Then there is the other side of the coin . . . really dumb choices of circumstances. Let's look at a few.

There was little doubt that the man would probably have been the Democratic party's nominee for president of these United States and would have had an excellent chance of taking the oath for that highest of offices. Most of the poll results and the political pundits seemed to agree on that. And then, in an incredibly stupid (there is no other descriptor) choice of contextica, he placed himself in a cruise boat docked by a Caribbean island in the company of a woman not his wife at a time when he was a highly scrutinized candidate for president! Gary Hart's plausible dream was quickly ended in a maelstrom of public indignation from which he could never recover politically. Now working in the private sector as an attorney, he must rue the day he allowed himself to be in circumstances where he certainly should not have been. Really bad time and place.

The presidential aspirations of another were dashed in yet another classic example of wittingly placing oneself in the wrong place at the wrong time. Partying 'til the wee hours of the morning and being in a car with a young woman (same scenario — not his wife) froze Ted Kennedy's political climb to the presidency at the senatorial level. It also brought unwanted international renown to the then unknown island of Chappaquiddick. The tragic drowning of his campaign aide cemented the time and place aspects of the incident which no spinmeister could disguise. Kennedy's image as a member of a family of courageous public servants was tarnished forever. Image results from contexts. Bad contexts . . . bad images.

### *The Beloved Princess*

The world mourned the untimely death of Diana, Princess of Wales, who left two children motherless because of clearly avoidable contexts. Unwisely getting into a limousine late at night with a driver and passengers of questionable sobriety and engaging in a high speed race with other vehicles was a horrible contextual mistake for which the ultimate price was exacted. Who was chiefly to blame for the tragedy may never be known, but all the occupants of the limo were mature adults who placed themselves, or allowed themselves to be placed, in harm's way.

* * * * * * * *

Would Robin Cook be the famed author he is if he had not been assigned to that submarine? Would Phil Donahue be the icon of talk show hosts, if he had not changed locations? Would Mitzi Ross have met her desired mate without her plan? Perhaps . . . perhaps not.

Would Gary Hart and Ted Kennedy have achieved the highest office in the land, had they given greater attention to their contextual choices? We'll never know. Princess Diana's tragic end was, however, clearly attributable to unfortunate contexting. Context *is* everything . . . even a matter of life or death. All of us in hindsight — which, is always 20/20 (I do *like* cliches . . . they usually impart some enduring wisdom) — can probably look back over our lives and remember places we should not have been and we now regret having been there.

**"Everybody's gotta be someplace!"**

There is the old joke about the hapless fellow who got caught in a woman's bedroom. Accosted by an angry husband who demanded to know what he was doing there, he lamely replied: "Everybody's gotta be someplace!"

Ex-president William Clinton — despite the experience of his idol, John Kennedy — chose to fool around in the worst of all contexts . . . the Oval Office in the people's house. Any other "someplace" would have been much less damaging to his presidency.

One of my friends, into online day-trading with his new computer, consistently seems to buy stocks at the wrong time (when the price is high) and sell them at another wrong time (when the price is low). While we can't always foresee what may or may not happen — luck, destiny, fate, conditions beyond our control all play a part — we should have a strategy for helping us to make the best decisions, to be good contexters. That strategy is to develop our creativity . . . the awesome resource we *all* have . . . so that we position ourselves consistently to be in the right places at the right times.

My earnest wish is that the next chapters will lead you to that goal and to the enjoyment of a more dynamic and creative life filled with wonder, excitement and fulfillment.

***Now . . . let's get to it!***

## Chapter Three

# CREATIVE THINKING

## Part One

**"The mind of man (and woman) is bounded only by the universe."**
**— unknown**

Perhaps by now you're pretty much convinced that the surroundings we're in and the times we choose are of crucial importance in shaping our lives, and that we can change those contexts for the better. If you're not . . . then go back and reread chapters one and two. No, no! Just kidding again. Truth probably is that you knew most of the foregoing and the reading has just served as a reminder. In succeeding chapters we'll look at spatio-temporal contexts and their relation to schooling, work, social relationships, money, and some other areas. But for now let's give attention to how we can unleash that marvelous resource we all possess called creativity.

Our contexts are constantly changing. This is an unalterable fact of life. It is the human condition. Birth, death, marriage, divorce, job relocation, health, aging, retirement and a myriad of other factors ensure that we truly can never "swim in the same river twice." Each day we are different from the preceding day. The purpose here is to impress that we can and should exert *more* control over our contexts in relation to those inevitable changes. But it is pointless to make changes just for the sake of change. No, we should want to strive for new, exciting and rewarding changes. In one hilarious cartoon (*The Lockhorns),* the wife of the constantly-sparring duo tells her husband as they're watching the tube: "We're in a rut, Leroy. Let's move the TV to the other corner." New dynamic and meaningful changes can be achieved if we use the creative thinking power that is in all of us. Unfortunately, most of us don't begin to tap that unique potential we all have. It is very important to first explore why this is so and then continue on to how we can use proven strategies to creatively context our lives.

Let's begin this exploration with a little exercise. Even if you're not enthused about puzzles or games, please take time to do this one. It's important and will be referred to in several places throughout the book. It makes a good point and only takes a fun minute.

***The Nine Dots***

**CONNECT ALL NINE DOTS, USING FOUR STRAIGHT LINES WITHOUT LIFTING YOUR PENCIL FROM THE PAPER.**

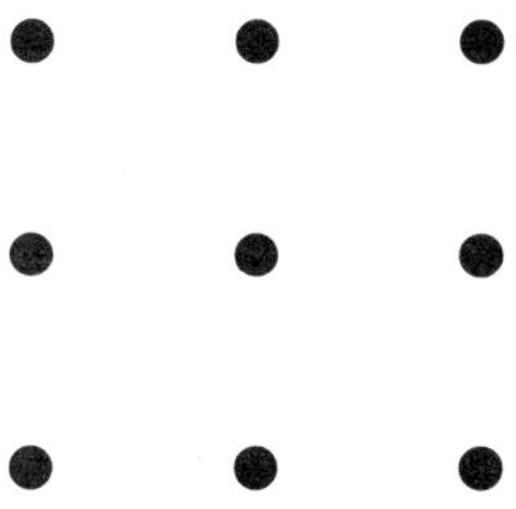

**(Solution is at the end of this chapter . . . don't peek!)**

Frustrated? Unsuccessful? Can't be done, you say? Or maybe you've solved the problem without prior knowledge. If so, skip this section . . . you've already captured the message of these pages. But don't leave. This can be a refresher course for you. Besides, there are many more pages I've taken the trouble to write and you've already invested some time in reading this far, so you may as well go the whole route. It's the polite thing to do and you're a polite person. How do I know that? People who read books are from a civil, courteous breed. Check it out at a library. Ever see anyone there yelling or sponging in line at the checkout counter? Nah. But we digress . . . let's get back to the future.

If you couldn't connect the nine dots with four straight lines, go now to the end of the chapter for the solution. I'll wait

..........................................................................................................................

..........................................................................................................................

..........................................................................................................................

..........................................................................................................................

.........................................*signifies waiting*.........................................................

..........................................................................................................................

..........................................................................................................................

..........................................................................................................................

O.K. You're back and probably feeling a little perturbed, slightly embarrassed or even cheated. Maybe you feel a little foolish. Don't. If you couldn't solve it, you're in the company of 90% of people (including me) who were frustrated. We had a self-imposed restriction that we were to stay within the nine-dot field and as long as we held that false impression, the solution was impossible. We were inmates in our self-made nine-dot prisons. To achieve a solution we *had* to go beyond the field and to a wider context. Once we understood that the outer space was available to us, the problem was easily solved.

The lesson to be learned from our little puzzle, as you may have anticipated by now, is that our lives need not be dictated by our present circumstances. We have the ability in a free society to go beyond our imaginary limitations in order to achieve better, more fulfilling lives. We need not be frozen in contexts which may be unsatisfactory — or even worse: debilitating, harmful or dangerous. The exercise also affords an excellent working definition of creativity. Creative thinking, subsequently referred to as CT, builds upon and supplements logical thinking. CT is taking that "road less traveled." It's breaking the mold, getting out of the rut, looking for new, different, original solutions to problems, going *beyond* the confining nine-dot field. The history of the advancement of our civilization is really the history of CT. From humankind's first use of crude tools to today's amazing computers, someone had to think of a new, original way of making or doing something differently. Look around you . . . all you see with only two exceptions I can think of — your body and the air around you — are the results of the CT of legions of your peers and predecessors. If you're reading this outdoors add land, water, other creatures, and heavenly bodies to the exceptions. *All* other things around us are the results of the wonderful workings of a marvelous organ.

### *The Human Brain*

***"It's three extraordinarily glorious, marvelous, almost miraculous pounds of meat."***
***— Patricia Smith Churchland, Neurophilosopher***

When Bill Moyers interviewed Dr. Churchland, whose career has been devoted to the study of the human brain, he closed the session with a very incisive and thought-provoking comment: "It is absolutely astounding to me that an *organ* can attempt to understand itself!" Our brains are certainly the most wondrous of all things in existence. Consider that as you read this, what is going on is that one organ (mine) is communicating with another organ (yours). Your arms are holding the book so that your eyes can relay the symbols on the page to your brain for its interpretation of the stimuli. Your eyes and arms and the rest of you can all be viewed as simply accessories or servants of the brain. As I review these words on the computer screen, it is really an organ (my brain) interacting with *itself*! Truly astounding!

Paul Broca's seminal work in the mid-nineteenth century laid the groundwork for more recent brain anatomists to establish that certain functions exist in specific areas of the brain. Our ability to speak is controlled by a small spot in the third convolution of the left frontal lobe of the cerebral cortex. The late, great Carl Sagan refers to our having two brains in one skull in that the two hemispheres have different functions. It is now generally accepted that the "left brain" has more to do with logical, sequential analysis while the "right brain" is the seat of our creative potential. Edward DeBono tells us, amusingly, that vertical thinking (left brain) is concerned with digging the same hole deeper, while lateral thinking (right brain) is concerned with digging the hole somewhere else. The term "convergent thinking" is associated with the former and "lateral thinking" is synonymous with creativity. Trying to solve our nine-dot puzzle by staying within the field may be likened to digging deeper in a hole, while going beyond the area (digging other holes) represents creative or divergent thinking.

Some writers in the field of CT perhaps make too much of the left brain/right brain phenomenon as if convergent and divergent thinking were arch enemies. Public schools are often criticized for being concerned only with developing convergent thinking skills. Those critics point to the inherent curiosity and vivid imaginations of preschool children which are then stifled in classrooms where the emphasis is on discipline, conformity, following the rules and getting one correct answer.

The two thinking processes are not mutually exclusive but are, rather, complementary. Of course we need to think logically and we do need discipline and rules. Otherwise chaos would prevail. CT, divergent thinking, creative problem-solving — all used interchangeably here — come into play as partners not adversaries. Creative solutions, no matter how "far out" they may seem, become logical after they have demonstrated worth. While it is true that schools must give most of their attention to convergent thinking, there has been a dramatic increase in fostering CT in America's classrooms. A threat to this trend is that in our desperate efforts to improve achievement test scores, memorization of facts will take precedence over developing thinking skills. Good teachers of any subject area and at any grade are aware of the need to infuse creativity in their instruction . . . to nurture <u>both</u> hemispheres of the brain, so that it can perform its most important function — thinking.

**Convergent and divergent thinking are complementary . . . they are partners.**

***Activated Catenated Psychosynapsis***

Jack Taylor, author of *How to Create New Ideas*, offers the above as a definition of thinking.

In less pedantic (Does just using this word make one guilty of pedantry?) words, it simply means moving messages around in the head. Doing that has, of course, resulted in a twenty-first century planet earth whose inhabitants seem able to do just about anything. The science fictions of Leonardo da Vinci (submarines, helicopters, etc.) are science facts today. The idea that one would be able to see and hear anything going on in any part of the world via television was preposterous just sixty years back. At that time, planning to send earthlings to the moon would have evoked a "Yeah, right." Just a few years ago, the idea of a potency pill (Viagra) would have been considered a joke. Things considered "far out" today may be totally "in" some tomorrow. Considering the advancements made in so many fields of human endeavors in the last two hundred years — a nanosecond of humankind's existence — what will happen in the next two hundred years will be awesome . . . probably beyond comprehension today. It now seems valid to say that anything we can imagine, we can accomplish. All because of activated catenated psychosynapsis

**Anything we can imagine, we can accomplish.**

What is also amazing is that our civilization has progressed so well and so quickly — a great majority of all the stuff we use every day has been developed within the last hundred years — *with only a small percentage of people doing the thinking.* Most of us, most of the time, do not begin to use the thinking powers we have. Research suggests that we use only ten to fifty percent of our creative potential. It has been flippantly, but aptly, said that:

> *Five percent of people think, five percent think they think, five percent will think if they have to, and the rest would rather die than think.*

A sad state of affairs indeed! But, why is this so? Let's explore some of the reasons we don't activate our catenated psychosynaptic system nearly as much as we can and should.

### *Couch Potato Contexts*

Enjoying the pleasures and benefits of an affluent and technologically gifted society is a glorious blessing but it has exacted a very high price in a tremendous and pathetic waste of human potential. With a hundred plus channels to surf through and the click of the remote, it is so easy to settle back on the couch and while away precious hours. Not that TV doesn't have many redeeming features, it certainly does, but the time the average American sits passively — estimated at an average six hours per day — in front of the tube displaces valuable thinking time. The wonderful world of television is an arch enemy of creativity. It takes a lot of will power to control its insatiable appetite. Six hours is one-fourth of our daily allotment! If Archimedes, Galileo, Shakespeare, Jefferson, Pasteur, Carver, Salk, Einstein, etc. had a similar diversion, we would probably still be in the dark ages.

There are other kinds of potato examples which discourage us from thinking. There is the *golf cart potato* who will chase that little white ball for countless hours and days and then wonder how people find time to do anything. Scotland, where golf originated, passed a law in 1457 prohibiting its people from playing the game because the Parliament felt time was taken away from another pursuit deemed more important — military training. There is the *sports fan* ( a word well derived from "fanatic" ) *potato* whose life rises or falls with the fortunes of a group of grossly overpaid athletes. There are also: *movie show potatoes, video rental potatoes*, and

— a close cousin to the couch — *recliner potatoes*. The term *"mouse potato"* has made it to the latest Oxford Dictionary warning us that even the wonderful computer can be a liability. Surfing the web or the Internet chat rooms can be voracious time wasters.

It's up to us as to our use or abuse of those great inventions. We earn the title of "potato" when any of those take *too* large a part of our time. Whether we like it or not, we all — rich or poor, young or old, black or white — get the same exact twenty-four hour a day allowance. Where we place ourselves in that time context determines who we will be. Going any of the Idaho routes is an escape mechanism that gives substance to that charge that many of us would rather die than think. CT's worst enemies are the various couch syndromes. Let's look at some more.

**The Hamburger King**

The late Ray Kroc, founder of McDonald's — one of the greatest success stories of our time — attributed ninety percent of achievement to motivation. He deemed it much more important than intelligence. With that philosophy he looked for people with drive to be his management team and franchise owners. He believed that no matter how smart or educated one may be, nothing will be accomplished until the body is set in motion. A highly motivated employee with an average I.Q. would be preferable to a lazy genius. Lack of motivation — closely related and caused by the various potato syndromes — is the killer of dreams.

There is the parable of the young rabbit who fell into a large, deep hole and after many frantic attempts could not get out. He called to another rabbit, "I can't get out . . . go get help!" His friend complied, returning several minutes later with some adult rabbits whereupon they found the victim hopping merrily towards them. "What happened, I thought you couldn't get out?" "I couldn't . . . but then a very large snake slithered down and I **had** to!" replied the survivor.

A few years ago, a lone construction worker was pinned under a large sewer pipe which had rolled onto his leg. A passerby, a man in his mid-seventies, tried to lift the heavy pipe off and was finally able to do so after two unsuccessful efforts. Rescue workers arrived and were amazed at the older man's feat. Two burly young men could not budge the pipe. When they asked the septuagenarian how he had done it, his reply: "he was in awful pain, I **had** to do it."

The successes of both the rabbit and the older rescuer were due to very strong external motivators . . . the need to save life. But in our quest for self-fulfillment and the maximization of our potentials, we must rely on ourselves for motivation. It's great to have had encouraging teachers and supportive parents — and many a spouse has been credited with a wife's or husband's achievements — but the buck stops with you. Lack of motivation . . . another villain of CT.

## Habitual Offenders

Next in the line-up of anti-CT culprits is the powerful force that habits play in our lives. We become very comfortable with our habits and in many ways that is good. Once we learn how to bicycle or drive an automobile by consciously directing our muscles to make the right moves, it soon becomes an automatic set of responses. We cultivate the good habits of brushing our teeth after meals, going to church, following rules of etiquette, exercising regularly, etc. These well-established activities save us time if we don't have to think about how to do them on every occasion. We are, very much so, creatures of habit. A quick example:

> Fold your arms in front of your chest. Chances are a zillion to one that you folded them in the same way you always have . . . the right arm going under your left wrist and your right hand resting on your left bicep . . . or vice versa. Now, fold them the opposite way. Feels awkward, doesn't it? If you do it the latter way several times, it'll become more familiar.

The way you fold your arms is certainly not of earthshaking importance. It's just an example of how habitual we are and that habits can be changed. Here's a case of where an automatic response to a sign needed a change of habit.

> A man encountered a street sign which said "one way only." He made an immediate about-face and proceeded in the opposite direction. It was after a few seconds that he realized . . . he was on foot!

Bad habits can keep us "in a rut," which is markedly different from being "in the groove."

Another habitual offender is mental set. Like habits — which we usually associate with physical behavior — mental sets are automatic psychological reactions to stimuli. Again, that can be good or bad. It's mostly bad for fostering creative behavior. We had a mental set which prevented us (most of us) from solving the nine-dot puzzle. Prejudices are undesirable mental sets. We see a person of another race and assume certain characteristics for that individual. We develop a set for dealing with problems. When a different problem comes along that requires a new type of solution or approach , we often have

**Being "in a rut" is markedly different from "being in a groove."**

trouble because we try to apply solutions that have worked in the past — and we get nowhere. This is a dangerous inhibitor of CT.

### "It'll Never Work!"

So far we've looked at time-wasting contexts, lack of motivation, and the force of habit as inhibitors of CT. Another member of the lineup is *repression*. Society tends to frown upon those who are different from the norm. As a result, many people make no effort to be creative, fearing that they will be looked down upon. After all, everyone loves to criticize. We're all familiar with:

**"Are you trying to be different?"**
**"Listen . . . you just do your job and let us do the thinking."**
**"That's crazy, it'll never work."**
**"Of all the nutty ideas you've dredged up, this is the absolute worst!"**
**"Conform . . . fit in . . . quit dreaming."**
**"Shape up . . . or ship out!"**
**"Get with the program."**
**"Don't rock the boat."**

Henry Ford had trouble getting engineers to work on his first assembly line because they all *knew* that it couldn't be done. And when the Xerox copying process was invented, it wasn't until four years later that someone decided to invest in it. An invention we now take for granted was proved to be impossible. A group of eminent physicists and other experts of the time period, after many years of study, proved scientifically that the inventor could never make his idea work. They decreed that it was absolutely incompatible with the then well known law of conversion of energy and even after it had functioned *and was placed in common usage*, there was still a group of scientists in Europe who maintained it absolutely couldn't work. The inventor was Edison . . . the invention, the light bulb.

The most creative people on earth are children. To them the world holds an endless fascination . . . it is a giant playground for their imaginations. Then, as an infant, the societal pressure starts. The word "no" is ingrained in the baby's mind as soon as communication begins. "No . . . don't touch, that's hot!" As children, there are the parents' admonitions to "keep out of the cabinets, put that away, look at the mess you're making." Schools follow, necessarily insisting on conformity and discipline: change classes at the appointed time, stand in line, memorize this subject matter, follow this procedure . . . etc.

No wonder that thinking for ourselves is so difficult, which may have prompted this acerbic comment from Adlai Stevenson when he ran against Dwight D. Eisenhower for president. Someone came up to him after he finished a campaign speech to tell him he would have "the support of all thinking Americans." "Not enough," Stevenson replied. "I'm going to need a majority."

Of course, much of the above is a desirable and essential part of an individual's development into a sane and civilized society. But the point is that we must now put our repressions, which have served their purposes, in the proper perspective so that they don't dampen or extinguish creative endeavors. Given these very powerful and longstanding influences, this is not an easy task — repressing repressions — but it is doable! It is well worth the effort.

We'll now go on to learning some techniques we can use to help us break free of all the inhibitors we've reviewed. The methods are all well researched, widely used for decades and have proved very effective in solving just about any problem of the human condition.

**Solution to the nine-dot puzzle:**

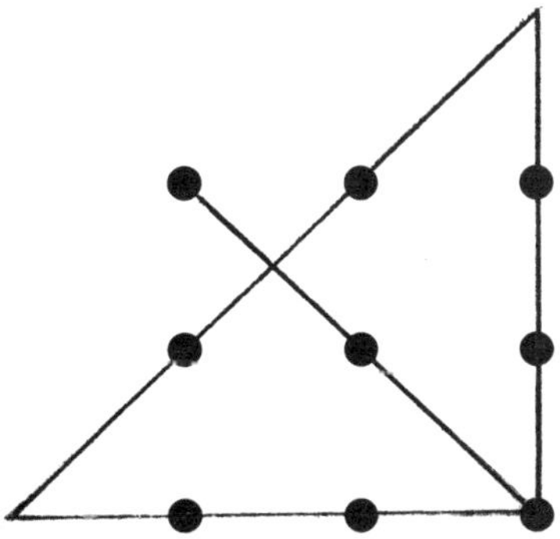

## Chapter Four

## CREATIVE THINKING

### Part Two

**"One of the prime elements of human uniqueness is the ability to create and exercise new options."**
**— Norman Cousins**

This book is a joint venture for both of us. More than just that I wrote it and you're now reading it. As with the nine-dot puzzle and the arm-folding, every now and then you'll be asked for your participation, your interaction. These exercises have been carefully selected to: make a point; give insight; stimulate your imagination; and provide some practice in bringing out your creative potential. You may skip them, but if you do you'll be missing out on some valuable experiences as well as some fun. If you are serious about developing your CT, then please do them in earnest.

By way of introduction to the wonderful world of creativity, please:

> On a sheet of paper write down as many uses as you can think of for the common household broom *other* than sweeping. List as many as you can in one minute (give or take a few seconds). Total your responses.

(Do the above now . . . now is always the best of times. I'll wait.)

You've just taken a pre-test to measure IDEATIONAL FLUENCY. Whether you came up with two or ten other possible uses for a broom or drew a blank doesn't matter at this point. You will — after finishing this chapter — come up with two, three or four times as many responses. I promise you that . . . a quantum leap. Ideational fluency is simply the number of ideas one can think of on a particular problem or topic without any regard for their practicality at that point. It is a marvelous technique for creative contexting.

### *The More . . . The Merrier*

But what exactly, are ideas? They're thoughts, theories, intuitions, hunches, etc. Ideation is essentially synonymous with thinking. Let's just settle for the equation:

***production of ideas = creative thinking***

Shakespeare's Hamlet, Einstein's theory, Frost's *Mending Wall* are all ideas. "Wait a minute," you might be thinking right now. "I'm not a genius. How could I ever write a world-famous play, compose a great poem, find a cure for cancer, invent a space rocket or any of those things?" Actually, that's not the point. There are millions and millions of ideas around you . . . you are the epicenter of a world full of ideation. Not all of them are earthshaking, but ideas nevertheless. Writing a letter, choosing a movie, deciding where to go on vacation — are all ideas. My writing and your reading of this book are ideational processes. Any device you can think of, any piece of music, any machine, any thing in print . . . started out as an idea in someone's mind. Developing your ideational fluency involves coming up with as many possibilities as you can think of on a given problem without any regard as to the quality of the response. What is important is the quantity of responses . . . the more, the better. The well-supported theory is that the more options or ideas one can list, the greater the chance of ending up with the best choice. No addition to the list is ridiculous, crazy, unworkable, unrealistic, impractical or impossible. All judgement and criticism is withheld until after the listing is as complete as possible. Ideas first . . . evaluation later. Assessment must always be subsequent, never concurrent. Think of the idea-proliferation process as the flow of hot water . . . hot ideas. Allowing the cold water of criticism to be turned on, results in a lukewarm outcome.

Ideational fluency is the cornerstone of "brainstorming" — a group process of problem solving developed by Alex Osborne back in the 50's and used extensively in business and industry, think tanks and creativity classes today. Originally, groups of about fifteen people would compile lists of as many solutions to a given problem that they could come up with. There was a presenter and a recorder for each group. Responses were written on large flipcharts for all to see as the session progressed. Criticism was verboten . . . wild thinking called "freewheeling" was encouraged. The goal: to get the longest list possible. "Hitchhiking" was an important aspect. One response would elicit a related, yet different, additional possibility. Good teachers today use brainstorming or variations of it in their classes. Businesses rely on it to come up with new ideas for products or services.

Alas, neither you nor I can convene a brainstorming group of ten or fifteen people to help make a decision or solve a problem for us. But we can adapt the process. Talking with friends, relatives, confidantes, fellow workers, spouses . . . even strangers can aid in building a large list of possibilities. Doing some research at the library or on your computer will further enhance your list. You'll be amazed at how many ideas you'll garner. One idea will generate another . . . and then another . . . and so on. The more the merrier (and smarter). Remember, we are striving for quantity which will then lead to an ultimate quality.

There are times when we really don't want to spend hours or days researching or talking to anyone about a decision to be made. Maybe we need to solve some problem by six o'clock tonight! We can still utilize the principle involved by PERSONAL BRAINSTORMING. We simply sit down or lie down (my preference) and think about all the ideas we can come up with. The most important thing to remember when doing that is to record your thoughts. Get out that pencil and paper, your laptop or a tape recorder and list everything. There are three very compelling reasons for recording:

1. **Akin to the law of physics, no two thoughts can occupy the same space at the same time. Relying on your memory can too easily be your forgettery (yes, Spellchecker, I know there's no such word). Ideas are like fickle swains . . . they come and go very quickly.**

2. **We are then adding multisensory and motor components, getting our eyes and our ears (if tape recording) and our muscles involved. Memory experts tell us that the best way to remember something is to use the mnemonic device of association with other things. You're introduced to someone. You want to remember her name — which is Jacqueline Browning. You think: my favorite aunt's name is Jacqueline and she is an aspiring writer (Browning). Voila! Her name is Jacqueline Browning! One might question: why add all that stuff . . . why not just memorize the two words? Because, psychologists tell us, increasing the number of cues (associations) will increase our chances of recalling the name. It really works.**

3. **One of the strengths of group brainstorming is hitchhiking . . . latching onto someone else's thought to come up with a new one. We lose that resource when we are solo. When we record our thoughts and then review them, we can often hitchhike on our own ideas making up somewhat for the absence of interpersonal cross-pollination.**

At this point you may be thinking: "O.K., I understand that the more ideas or possibilities one can list, the better the chance of ending with a final good decision . . . ideational fluency . . . I'll buy it. But how can I come up with many ideas when much of the time I'm lucky to generate one or two or, worse, draw a blank?" Ah, there's help on the way. We're going to now look at some proven strategies which will be invaluable as kicks to our creative pants. So put those slacks on and let's get going!

### *There Is Nothing New Under the Sun*

Well . . . yes and no to that old expression. It is difficult, perhaps well nigh impossible, to come up with anything that is totally and completely new and original. Rather, all of the achievements we have today are really the results of the building upon or rearrangement of ideas from countless numbers of thinkers before us who found new ways of looking at existing things. In our ethnocentrism we like to think of the Wright brothers as the inventors of human flight although many Europeans had already laid much of the groundwork. There were hot-air balloonists and gliders long before Orville and Wilbur came on the scene. Centuries before, Leonardo daVinci had sketched the precursor to today's helicopter. Again, all the English literature ever written is simply differing arrangements of twenty-six letters of our alphabet; all music composed is a variation of eight basic notes; and, all the art masterpieces represent mixtures of just seven colors. So, much if not all of idea-finding is simply generating different combinations of existing things. Coming up with an idea which may not be original or unique at all is wonderful if it is original for the individual. Television stations — preparing their viewers for the inevitable summer reruns — blare: "if you haven't seen it, it's new for you." This is true. Let's now look at a really great way to increase your ideational fluency by making new associations between things . . . by recombining. It's called FORCED RELATIONSHIPS.

This technique involves contemplating what would happen if two (or more) seemingly totally unrelated things are pushed together to result in a new entity. The "things" might be products, ideas, processes, thoughts, theories . . . just about anything. Imagining the consequences of making new combinations is a definition of forced relationships. Examples of this abound all around you. Classical symphonies and rock music . . . how far apart can you get? Emerson, Lake and Palmer was just one group of many who have combined the two successfully.

Remember Mitzi Ross? She related the routine daily activity of lunch with searching for a mate. And how about Yenta, the matchmaker in *Fiddler on the Roof*, who made her living forcing relationships? John Gray's clever and catchy title for the bestselling *Men are from Mars, Women are from Venus* exemplifies an association of astrology and advice about relationships. Forcing weightlifting and jogging together gives us the runner who carries small dumbbells while racing by us. The things we use are the results of a series of forced relationships. The clock, the radio, the telephone have all been joined. Once separate entities, we now have the clock-radio-telephone. Not to be outdone, the computer manufacturers now offer the printer, copier, fax and scanner — all in one unit. Very near reality is the complete morphing of the computer with the telephone and television. What a menage a trois that will be!

Recently I had the good fortune of spending a couple of days at the Breakers Hotel in Palm Beach, Florida. Their buildings have the most beautiful ceilings of anywhere in the world. The artistry of American Michelangelos was adapted for their awesome overhead decor. Picture paintings are usually reserved for walls but force-fitting to the ceiling created a unique treasure.

Another demonstration of the clever forcing of relationships came on the beach there. I had planted my chair not far from a fellow sunbather who was reclining on a chaise lounge. He was talking on his portable phone. I couldn't help but overhear (well, maybe I could have, but I was interested) that all his calls were business-related. He would finish a conversation with one and then promptly ring up another. I stayed about an hour and when I left, he was still doing his "work" from his sun, surf and sand office. Combining work and pleasure . . . is that creative contexting, or what!

Some clever people at McDonald's looking to increase sales must have used the technique in deciding to seek new contexts for their hamburger heavens. Originally, they constructed freestanding buildings under those golden arches. Now, however, you'll find them in malls, airports, military bases and even schools. Their latest: forging partnerships with gasoline service stations. In what may have been considered a few years ago as unlikely alliances, they are now thriving joint enterprises. Few new gasoline service stations are built today that do not have a relationship with a convenience store or a fast food franchise . . . or both.

American manufacturing corporations have been forcing new relationships with foreign countries for the last three decades. Hundreds have moved their plants and distribution centers to faraway locations. The re-contexting enabled them to cut costs dramatically by substituting high-priced American labor with low-cost workers. This change-of-context movement is not new. Its precursor was the massive shift of factories from the North to the South following World War II. Prior to 1950, almost all automobile passenger tires made in the U.S.A. were from Akron, Ohio. By 1975, not a single automobile passenger tire came out of the "rubber city!" Lower cost labor and a union-free environment made several southern states the new homes for Goodyear, Firestone, et al. What is beneficial for a corporation (forcing new relationships, re-contexting) may also be good for an individual. That's what these pages are all about.

### *The Boy, the Bridge, and the Eighteen-Wheeler*

Perhaps you've heard this story. I haven't been able to authenticate it but that doesn't really matter as the point is effectively made whether it is fact, fiction, or even Truman Capote's "faction."

> A large semi-trailer truck was driven under a bridge which was not high enough for the eighteen-wheeler to pass through. It wedged itself between the bridge and the roadway and "all the king's horses and all the king's men" couldn't push the truck through or pull it back out. Tow trucks were of no avail and a call was sent out for a crew with several acetylene torches to cut part of the trailer's roof out. Among the onlookers was a ten-year-old boy who exclaimed, "why not just let the air out of the tires?" This fell upon receptive ears and the tire deflations began. Aided by the tow truck and the hapless vehicle's engine in reverse, the monstrous rig was finally freed.

This account or anecdote — whatever — leads us to another easy-to-use technique for fostering CT. It's called CHECKLISTING. There have been many checklists developed through the years (Eberle, DeBono, Taylor, et al.) designed to trigger new ideas. Robert Eberle's *Scamper* was utilized by hundreds of teachers in elementary grade classes throughout the country. Our youngster — who came up with the clever stuck-truck solution — could well have been one of the beneficiaries of such creative instruction.

Perhaps the original model for most lists is that devised by Alex Osborne in his classic book, *Applied Imagination*. His checklist uses a series of verbs to spur new ideas. Variations of his format have been developed by many others but his remains as a model.

**Adapt**

**Combine**

**Eliminate**

**Magnify, minify, modify**

**Put to other uses**

**Reverse, rearrange**

**Substitute**

Osborne not only found that applying his checklist to just about any problem produced valuable ideas, but he was elated in noting that peoples' attitudes changed when they practiced the process repeatedly. They developed a greater confidence in themselves and became more open-minded. Not a bad byproduct.

CHECKLISTING can be used in just about *any* problem-solving situation. Applying clever Mitzi Ross's strategies of how to find a suitable life partner, we can see that she effectively *combined* her lunch site with a favorable place to meet men. She regularly *put* (her lunch hour) *to other uses*. She *rearranged* her routine to achieve a goal. Mitzi *magnified* her opportunities by going to both the medical and law libraries. Writers use the method to create novel plots or different characters. Superman with his *magnified* strength, the countless *adaptations* of Shakespeare's plays, *reversing* time as in the *Back to the Future* movies are examples. The brilliant Pulitzer-Prize-winning humor of Dave Barry is based on incongruous exaggerations (*magnifications*).

The technique is apparent in virtually all new product development. Inventing or improving on something we use comes about by new combinations inspired by one or more of the verbs from Guilford's list. The word processor is a *combining* of the computer and typewriter which was an even greater leap than going from the pencil to the typewriter. The largest selling vehicles are now vans and wagons, which are *adaptations* of passenger cars and small trucks and we are now working feverishly to *adapt* stem cells for possible cures of several diseases. The inventor of the vacuum cleaner simply *reversed* the flow of air. Television receivers are *magnified* to forty, or more, inch screens or *minimized* to two inch portables. We have *put to other uses* the knowledge gained from the development of the atomic bomb. That awesome energy which was used to decimate Hiroshima and Nagasaki has been *minimized* to propel ships and submarines and to provide electricity for millions of homes.

Time for a little practice exercise. Keeping *CHECKLISTING* and *FORCED RELATIONSHIPS* in mind, come up with as many ideas as you can on this implausible (I hope) challenge:

> You've finished reading this book and have concluded that it was a complete waste of your valuable time. You don't want to save it for future reference or even pass it on to a friend. It was that bad! (An absurd conclusion in my humble and biased opinion.) Rather than just chucking it into the garbage, list all the ideas you can on what uses it can be put to.

We'll do this together for a couple of minutes using just two of Guilford's items (*CHECKLISTING* and *FORCED RELATIONSHIPS*). Feel free to hitchhike on my ideas. Remember, *nothing* is ridiculous or farfetched. We're going for quantity, not quality. Here we go.

***Put to other uses:*** ***. . . a doorstop . . . leaf press . . . paper weight . . . weapon***
***. . . toilet tissue (ugh!)***
***. . . storage file for photos, bills***
***. . . a safe for valuables by hollowing out the inside***
***. . . a posture aid; walking with it on your head***
***. . . a base to raise your computer monitor to eye level***
***. . . a fly swatter***
***. . . a step stool by combining it with other books***

***Modify:*** ***. . . pages by shredding to use as confetti or packaging fill***
***. . . tear out and roll pages into fireplace flame starters***
***. . . spread pages to catch paint drips***
***. . . use hard cover as a ruler or as glass coasters***
***. . . use the separated hardcover to disguise another book you're reading***

So there you have it. Almost twenty uses for this book besides its real function, which as you know, is to make you more aware — and more in control — of your very precious contextica. Again, never mind that some of the ideas seem ridiculous or absurd to you. Someone else may see a gem in what could be perceived as a lot of gravel by others. I wouldn't use hard covers of books as coasters, but I can envision an artsier-than-I person brushing on a coat of polyurethane and putting them on a coffee table and guests reacting with "how very clever."

CHECKLISTING and FORCED RELATIONSHIPS are two great ways of helping us to come up with those ideas which can solve <u>any</u> problem in <u>any</u> area of our lives.

Rather than relying on something to pop into our heads, the two methods give a neat framework for becoming more ideationally fluent and, consequently, better creative contexters.

The two techniques can also be used in a more formal and structural setting known by various experts in the field as MORPHOLOGICAL ANALYSIS or MATRIXING. This involves listing an array of possibilities or factors on horizontal lines and then listing another assortment of possibilities in vertical columns. Then a matrix is constructed which provides a cell for each of the relationships between the lines and columns. This is a two-dimensional model but one can also make it in three dimensions. Both are analytical, logical and sequential approaches which lead us to creative solutions. It is a comprehensive way to list and examine many possible combinations that might be useful in spurring ideation. The developers of the World War II V-2 rocket used morphological analysis as did Thomas Edison in achieving the hundreds of patents awarded to him. The process is not restricted to product design or invention but can be valuable in any area of human activity. Let's do this one as an example. I'll set it up . . . provide some prospective matches . . . then you apply it to your unique, personal situation. We'll use Osborne's checklist (*Adapt, Combine, Eliminate, Magnify, Other Uses, Reverse, Substitute*) as one dimension and important areas of our lives as the other.

First, here's what a blank format would look like.

| | Adapt | Combine | Eliminate | Magnify Minify Modify | Put to Other Uses | Reverse Rearrange | Substitute |
|---|---|---|---|---|---|---|---|
| Relations | | | | | | | |
| Home | | | | | | | |
| Education | | | | | | | |
| Work | | | | | | | |
| Finances | | | | | | | |
| Health | | | | | | | |
| Safety | | | | | | | |

There you have it! A great planning and self-inventory format to improve your life. Let's look at an example of how this technique could be used in a personal situation.

Cheryl Greene is unhappy with her job as a cosmetics salesperson for a large department store. The income is low, the fringe benefits are skimpy, and she's not ecstatic about the people with whom she works. Single at twenty-four, she's had no education beyond a high school diploma. Interested in physical fitness, Cheryl works out regularly at a local club and has a model's figure. Her face is typical of the ones you usually see at the Clinique or Estee Lauder counters . . . glamorously pretty. She feels unfulfilled in her present position . . . she's ready for a change.

Let's use the matrix to see how many possibilities we can generate by crossing these verbs with just four areas of her life: work, relationships, education and finances. We don't need to cram our ideas into each cell. It's easier to use the table as a guide for listing our thoughts on paper.

And away we go.

| | |
|---|---|
| *Adapt:* | ***Adjust to the present job by improving relations with co-workers.***<br>***Increase pay by working harder for bigger commissions, ask for a raise.***<br>***Vie for promotion to manager, district supervisor.***<br>***Read Dale Carnegie's How to Win Friends and Influence People.***<br>***Take courses on retailing at community college.***<br>***Think of all the good things about the job.*** |
| *Combine:* | ***Schedule work with taking courses, seeking vocational counseling.***<br>***Write a book or article on using makeup, keeping fit.***<br>***Use the workplace or the mall to meet new friends, see other job possibilities.***<br>***Open your own cosmetics store . . . start a fitness center in the mall.***<br>***Take a part-time job to supplement income . . . explore new vistas.*** |
| *Eliminate:* | ***Quit the job . . . give notice and seek other work.***<br>***Identify and change negative feelings towards others (customers, bosses).***<br>***Stop unnecessary spending which may be straining your paycheck.***<br>***Do away with bad habits which may be diminishing your quality of life.*** |

| | |
|---|---|
| *Magnify:* | ***Capitalize on your attractive appearance to explore other occupations such as modeling, acting, public relations. Enhance your job marketability by getting more education or other work..*** |
| *Put to other uses:* | ***Enlist in the Peace Corps.***<br>***(hitchhike) Join one of the armed forces.*** |
| *Reverse:* | ***Instead of going from home to work, have the work come to home —start a home business.*** |
| *Rearrange:* | ***Change your work schedule . . . work more hours . . . work less hours.*** |
| *Substitute:* | ***Switch job locations by transfer within the company or with a new employer.*** |

This schematic procedure for forcing relationships need not be just the merging of the column and line items. Anything can relate to anything. For instance, the column items can be combined. Working at Home affects Finances and also accords a greater measure of Health and Safety. That kind of interrelating could be helpful in determining whether or not to start a home enterprise. The two-dimensional matrix is a simple, easy-to-use procedure which really helps in coming up with unconventional ideas by pushing conventional factors together. It's of great value to someone in Cheryl's position by helping her to explore many more options in her quest for greater fulfillment.

A three-dimensional model affords many more possibilities. Consider how a writer of fiction might use it in searching for an idea for her next book or TV pilot.

One set of variables might be concerned with the types of plot, another with the characters, and the third with possible settings.

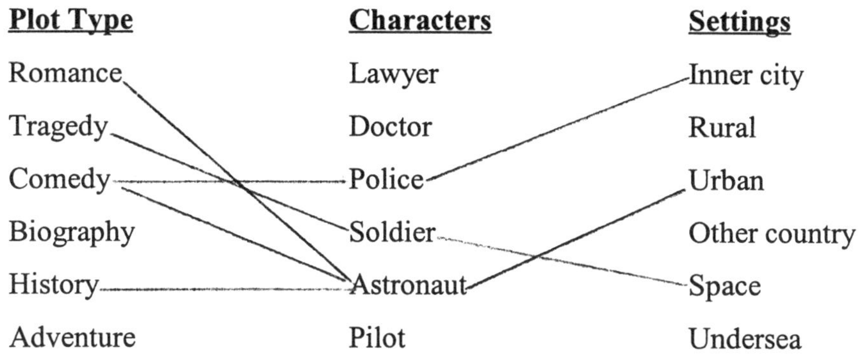


Perhaps a comedy about a policeman in the inner city? Or a tragedy about soldiers stranded in space? Or a historical, romantic comedy concerning alien astronauts landing in San Francisco during the Gold Rush? Remember, you can work within sets as well as between and among them. Obviously, the more items or factors you can come up with for the axes, the better. Assuming four items for a column and four items for lines in a two-dimensional format gives us sixteen cells for responses. (Of course, you are encouraged to put as many responses as you can in each cell.) Going to three dimensions — again assuming four items for each of the three planes — elicits sixty-four places for ideas.

Look at morphological analysis or matrixing somewhat the same as playing slot machines known aptly as "one arm bandits." Even though slot machines are now built with push buttons, the processes are the same. They've retained the arms, although few seem to crank them nowadays. How lazy can we get? Either way, in CT, you're trying for new combinations which will result in ideas for your life. With the slots, you're hoping a certain alignment of the wheels will bring a flow of cash. In both, if you do it long enough, you will "hit a jackpot!" Of course, you may go broke in Las Vegas (many do) but don't worry about running out of brain cells — you've got zillions of those.

***" Dreams are the royal road to the unconscious. "***
***— Sigmund Freud***

Yes, Dr. Freud, but dreams are also royal roads *within our consciousness*. Which brings us to the last of our strategies for becoming creative contexters. It's probably the most valuable of all if we quickly define it with its most positive connotations. Dreaming is: imagining, envisioning, conceiving, aspiring, fantasizing and desiring. Most if not all of our achievements started out as dreams. Since the word has its negative meanings (my thesaurus lists opposites for "dream" as "accomplishment" and "reality"), let's clarify what we mean here. We're talking about daydreaming, not about that mysterious activity that occurs during our sleep and about which we really know very little. We're concerned here with dreaming as FREE ASSOCIATION, which is really . . . thinking. In our reveries, we reflect about our fears and fantasies: we visualize the kitchen with new cabinets; imagine what life would be like in a different place; realize unfulfilled ambitions; and wish we would win the lottery and then fantasize on how we would spend the money. Free association is a wonderfully relaxing activity enabling us to go anywhere and do anything. Free association is invaluable in our quest for creativity. It is the easiest of all to use. You merely start with a thought (a problem, a word, a symbol, anything) and let your mind wander pondering that contemplation. You don't need to concentrate all that much on what you're doing. Just relax and more or less daydream about the train of thoughts that will inevitably start.

Advertising agencies have to rely on creative ideas for their clients. Here's one scenario where someone could have dreamed up just the right name for a new product:

> You work for an advertising agency and need to come up with a name for a new tire. Hmmm . . . tire . . . round . . . looks like a doughnut . . . a steel doughnut . . . solid, strong . . . hard as a rock . .. sturdy as a soldier . . . the tire of the century . . . tomorrow's super tire . . . That's it! It's the SuperSteel Centurion, from the Acme Tire Company.

This random thinking process eventually reaches the point of an "aha!" and that slap on the forehead which herald the joy of having produced a good idea. Daydreaming should be given more importance and time by most of us. Modern life, unfortunately, militates against this. Almost every minute of our day is controlled or occupied by someone else. Work, school, friends, spouses, children, watching television, surfing the Internet — all control what we think about. It's really essential that we regularly get away from it all and just kick back and let our minds roam.

Here's an example of doing just that . . . (a little humor break):

> A young man sitting in the aisle seat of a jet airliner was admiring a beautiful flight attendant as she walked back and forth doing her work. The plane suddenly hit an air pocket causing her to lose stability. As she sought to maintain balance, her arm flailed out and she accidentally slapped the passenger across the face. Embarrassed, she went into a profuse apology when he interrupted saying: "It's O.K., forget about it. I've been looking at you and for what I was thinking . . . I deserved the slap."

Free association may be practiced in two ways: formal and informal. Our young man in the foregoing anecdote exemplifies the informal kind in which we fantasize about anything . . . meeting the man or woman of our dreams, getting that promotion, gaining revenge, winning the lottery, traveling abroad, etc. In those reveries, we fulfill our wishes and desires in a virtual reality. In the recesses of our minds, we can be anyone and do anything! Truly an amazing phenomenon which provides a temporary escape, a refuge from a sometimes tension-filled existence. We all have our Walter Mitty sides and that is good.

For making decisions or solving problems, however, we need to structure the process so it will lead to some end. In formal free association, we identify a concern and focus on it. We also provide a means of remembering our thoughts by recording them. Pencil and paper, tape recorder, word processor — whatever you feel most comfortable with. The important thing is not to have your ideas lost to oblivion. Reviewing your notes in a subsequent free association session will give you more possibilities . . . the "hitchhiking" factor described earlier. Your mind recalls one image, word or speck of information and this leads to a recall of another . . . and another . . . and another. Reading (or listening to) our data enhances this proliferation process. Again — at the risk of being repetitively repetitive (?) — I urge you to record your free association sessions. This need not be done during the activity if it seems to disrupt the flow, but it should be accomplished as soon as possible. Dream (the night time kind) analysts tell us we can recall what we've dreamt if we, immediately, upon awakening, think about our nocturnal illusions. If we wait, our minds quickly turn to the business of the conscious world.

One of the little aggravations of our lives is when someone at one end of a phone conversation has to say: "Wait a minute until I get a paper and pencil." In our continuing search for a better life through creatively choosing the best contextica, it's really smart to put paper and pencil wherever you may be when ideation erupts: the bedroom night stand, by each telephone, next to your favorite couch or recliner, (when you use either of those two pieces of furniture for free associating, you're not a "potato") and, yes, in the "throne room" where privacy is sacrosanct. Also take them out to the porch or that hammock in the yard and certainly have them in your car. Maybe I'm pushing the envelope here but you may want to have a small pad and writing instrument available wherever you go — the symphony, to dinner, the ball game . . . even when you're out bicycling or jogging. A terrific thought can manifest itself at any time or place. If you don't make a capture, it will escape forever . . . maybe longer!

In summary, we've talked about: IDEATIONAL FLUENCY, PERSONAL BRAINSTORMING, FORCED RELATIONSHIPS, CHECKLISTING and FREE ASSOCIATION. There are other strategies for CT development, but most are really variations or combinations of these. Indeed, as you may have gleaned by now, the ones we've dealt with have quite a bit of overlapping. As you formally free associate about a topic, you may use a checklist as a point of departure. Free association is almost synonymous with personal brainstorming. Forced relationships and checklisting are close relatives. No need to compartmentalize them. Some of them work better with certain situations than others but usually a combination is involved. In succeeding chapters, we'll practice our skills for applying these techniques to important areas of our lives. As some preparation for that let's return to that broom pre-test you took at the beginning of this chapter. (You did take it, didn't you?) You remember I promised you'd double, triple or even quadruple your score? Well . . . this is the moment of truth! Now we apply CT to find how many other uses of the common household broom we can find. We'll use a checklist as an appropriate tool for this challenge. I said this book was a joint venture for both of us, so let's do the post-test together.

Our task was to list as many uses we could think of for the common broom — other than what it was designed for (sweeping floors). We had a minute limit. Here we go . . .

***Put to other uses:***

***. . . as a weapon to usher snakes, rodents out of house.***
***. . . as a symbol of victory (submarines, a clean sweep).***
***. . . spray it gold and give as trophy.***
***. . . spider web duster.***
***. . . Halloween costume prop (witch).***
***. . . spread asphalt sealer on driveways.***
***. . . as paint brush for garage floor, decks.***
***. . . poor kids' hockey sticks.***
***. . . an oar for a canoe . . . as a torch (dip bristle end in gasoline).***

***Modify:***

***. . . cut wood handle off and use as: pool cue, stick ball bat, sign stand, flagpole, pointer, baton, chinning bar, closet pole.***
***. . . paint tip white for use as a cane for blind person.***
***. . . use as a defensive weapon.***
***. . . weave bristles into place mats.***
***. . . use single straw to pick teeth.***

Whoops, our minute is up. How many did we get? Twenty is pretty good and we only used *two* of the checklist verbs. But you get the point — applying a strategy results in a greater number of possibilities. There must be a deferral of judgment. Nothing is ridiculous. Of course *you* wouldn't pick your teeth with a broom bristle ( I have ), but that may lead to some other thought. As you review your lists these other ideas will surely pop up. Spraying the entire broom a bright and beautiful gold and awarding it as a fun trophy to the employee-of-the-month of a cleaning company could generate other, but similar, uses. As one example: election day campaigners carrying brooms as they work the polling places trying to unseat the incumbents. Signs on the brooms declaring "sweep the bums out" would be a low-cost, attention-getting maneuver. Such hitchhiking occurs frequently as we practice these techniques. As you look around, much of what you see should elicit a recognition of one or more of strategies we've reviewed. Isn't that street sweeper a magnification of the broom? It's a combination of a truck and a broom. Whisk brooms, toothbrushes, eyelash painters are examples of minification.

**CT enables us to go beyond the nine dots.**

Integrating these principles of creative thinking into our lives enables us to go beyond the nine dots . . . to find that we can live fuller, richer, more productive lives . . . to enjoy a world full of challenges, wonders and excitement. Never has there been a better time to live when so many more options are available to us. In Alan Murray's *The Wealth of Choices*, the author remembers that only a couple of generations ago, there was just one phone company and three major car manufacturers. Compare today's regional mall to the mom and pop stores of your grandfather's era.

What an incredibly wonderful world we live in!

### *"Work Will Fill the Space Made Available for It"*
### *— Parkinson's Law*

In a world in which "nothing is certain . . . not *even* that nothing is certain," Parkinson's wisdom comes closest to being an absolute. James Taylor's work with pig-iron handlers in the 1920's ushered in the age of scientific management. The first "efficiency expert," he proved that workers could produce as much or more in a smaller time frame, given the right incentives. I found verification of this when, as a high-schooler, I took a summer job in a broom factory. Operating a giant machine which took bristles and stapled them into blocks of wood to make heavy push brooms, I was paid "piece work" rates. The more I produced, the more moolah I got. As an energetic seventeen-year-old, I was cranking out those sweepers at a prodigious pace. It wasn't long before a union steward took me aside and explained the facts of labor vs. management life. He gently explained that I was just there for the summer, but my fellow workers had to labor the year round. Looking at my production level, the company would surely raise the broom number to make the same amount of money. Made sense to me, so I agreed to make fewer brooms within the original time space.

**Have you ever seen a house where the garage was not full?**

When the baby boomer children of World War II veterans skyrocketed public school rolls necessitating average class sizes of thirty-five and more, teachers did the job admirably. Today, any class sizes over twenty-eight are "impossible to teach." Bringing the point closer to home — have you ever seen a house where the closets and garage are not filled to capacity? No matter how big a refrigerator we get, it never seems to be large enough.

Maybe this proclivity to fill whatever spaces are made available to us is more than just a human trait. Perhaps it is our destiny. Demographers tell us that the earth's population has tripled to almost six billion people in less than a century. Astronomers reveal a constantly expanding universe. It is a scientific certainty that our life-giving sun will burn itself out in a billion years or so. Fortunately for us, that gives us plenty of time to find other world contexts. That space station we're building out there now is a start.

What does Parkinson's astute observation have to do with our concern here of developing creative thinking skills? It is very relevant. The more we learn and apply of CT, the greater are our options in utilizing the space we have, or, recognizing when that space should be enlarged. Again, as with the nine dots, we had to enlarge our assumed space to solve the problem. Researchers working with laboratory animals have discovered that mice placed in large cages grew physically bigger than those placed in smaller confines. We too can become bigger mentally and creatively if we expand our mental "cages." As humans journeying through this "stream of consciousness" called life, we all have the freedom and opportunity to do our thing.

To briefly summarize this chapter, we've:

. . . defined CT as the production of new (new for the individual) ideas.

. . . maintained that all of us have creative potential which is rarely used.

. . . described some of the barriers to CT as: lack of motivation, habit, fear of ridicule, mental sets and misuse of time.

We've also studied the creative problem-solving techniques of: ideational fluency, checklisting, forced relationships, morphological analysis, and free association.

We'll now move on to how we can use creative contexting in major areas of our lives: relationships, money matters, vocation/avocation, health and safety. We will emphasize the time-place connections in each of those. Some chapters will include a self-assessment and a format or blueprint for applying what we've learned to our own individual situations. Again, please engage yourself in the exercises. They're short and straightforward and will be very helpful in getting the most out of this experience.

**Be a better wife, husband, parent, daughter, son; make new friends; enjoy finer sex; live longer and healthier; get more fun out of life. Managing your contextica can help do all of that.**

Be a better spouse, parent, daughter, son, child, pal? Gain new friends? Enjoy finer sex? Increase your income? Get a better job? Lead a healthier, safer life? Live longer? Have more fun? Creative contexting can't, of course, guarantee any of that but it *will* greatly enhance achieving your aspirations through deliberate, conscious and creative selection of right places and right times.

***Right on!***

## Chapter Five

# FOUR STEPS TO CREATIVELY CONTEXTING YOUR LIFE

**"It is never too late to be what
you might have been."
— George Eliot**

Step 1 . . . ***Self Analysis***. Is this as good as it gets?

Step 2 . . . ***Set Goals***. If you don't know where you're going, any road will get you nowhere.

Step 3 . . . ***Self Start.*** Giving yourself a creative kick in the pants.

Step 4 . . . ***Succeed.*** How sweet it is!

There you have it . . . the four S's of creatively contexting your life. If you apply this rather straightforward and simple strategy to your situations, I guarantee (why not?) that you'll be ecstatic with the outcome. You'll never again look at things in quite the same way. I really want more than anything for you to gain from our time together an appreciation of the tremendous power of creativity. While no book can tell you how to live your life — human behavior is far too complex for that — the purpose here is to give you a guide, a strategy, a blueprint for better living. But — like the fellow in this anecdote . . .

> The old man prayed regularly to God to please allow him to win the lottery. He was, after all, a good person and he promised to give some of the money to worthwhile causes. Exasperated, after weeks of prayers with no response, the old man desperately cried out he was in very dire straits and sorely needed the help right now. God's voice thundered down: "All right, Sam, I'll have you win the lottery but you'll have to do your part." "What," the old man responded. "I'll do anything!" God roared impatiently: "*Buy a ticket*!"

You, too, have to buy your ticket. Simply committing to the four S's will do it. A cliche is appropriate here: "You can lead a horse to water but you can't make him drink." Think of the four-step plan as a fountain you're being led to. Now it's up to you to do the drinking (thinking). I hope you're thirsty. Let's start.

## The first step: *Self Analysis*

This is the most important and challenging of the four steps. Seeking to find out if one is reasonably happy, satisfied, content, untroubled and/or comfortable in his or her present contextica requires an introspection which few of us undertake on a regular basis. There are areas of our lives, however, where we do make periodic assessments.

Orthodox Jews, Roman Catholics, taxpayers, automobile owners and dentists . . . what do they all have in common?

Many, many years ago in small villages, Jews observed Yom Kippur — the day of atonement — by assembling around a goat and praying for forgiveness of their sins. They would then symbolically divest their sins onto the goat and proceed to chase the animal, who carried the collective guilt of the villagers, out of the settlement. From that tradition we have derived the word “scapegoat.”

For centuries and to this day, Catholics participate in the sacrament of “confession.” On a weekly or monthly or some other interval the parishioner relates all sins committed (“since my last confession”) to a priest. Just as the goat cleansed the Jews of their misdeeds, so also does the confessor absolve the Catholic, providing a certain penance is fulfilled.

Each year we all have to undertake a self-analysis of the financial aspect of our lives for that April $15^{th}$ date with the Internal Revenue Service. How much money did I make? How was it spent? What is deductible? Do I get a refund . . . or how much do I owe? We all do this annual chore because we have to, lest we run the risk of spending some time in a federal slammer.

The new owner of an automobile gets a manual with his set of wheels which sets up regular times when certain maintenance functions must be done. Failure to do so may void the dealer’s warranty or, worse, result in breakdowns on the road. (Although my manual calls for oil changes every 6500 miles, we are constantly pressured by the — not surprisingly — lube shops to change every 3000 miles or 3 months, whichever is sooner.) Our beloved cars get our regular attention.

“See your dentist twice a year.” “Get an annual physical examination.” These are admonitions we strive to follow because we want to keep the pearly whites as long as possible and we also want our bodies to last forever.

The point (and, like the comedienne, I do have one) is that regularly scheduled assessments of our morality, our finances, our cars, our teeth and our bodies are valuable, constructive and beneficial. Similarly, we should give the same importance to periodically evaluating the contextica we are in. The rabbi or priest reminds us of spiritual self-assessment times, the IRS sends our tax forms to us right after Christmas (nice of them to wait 'til after the holiday), our manuals or a warning light on the dashboard tell us to get the flivver serviced, doctors' offices are very efficient in sending postcards to get us to make that appointment — but there is no one bugging us to routinely look at our circumstances, our contexts. Well . . . I'm going to do that right now.

The first part of the first step is to **schedule a regular time** which we'll call ***sessions with yourself.*** You sit down, lie down, (can also be done while you're walking, jogging, tuned out of a boring lecture or sermon — but definitely not when you're driving as I may be on the same road as you) and ask yourself these trenchant and incisive questions:

**Am I reasonably content, happy, satisfied, fulfilled:**

- **with my life in general? . . . and then more specifically . . .**
- **with my relationships: family, spouse, significant other, friends, co-workers?**
- **with my job, education, avocation?**
- **with my physical condition?**

These ***sessions with yourself*** should be held **faithfully** at designated times and given top priority.

Regularly taking stock of your life is as, or more important than brushing your teeth, filing that tax return, watching another football game or TV sitcom. Schedule the session for each month on a day you'll remember — perhaps the 1st or the 15th, or your birthday numbers. For me, my birth date — the 5th — is the cue for that monthly conference with myself. Usually the site is in that ultimate relaxing device called a hammock. If the weather doesn't allow that, then it's a recliner in the den.

So settled, I light up one of my once-weekly cigars and begin answering the questions posed above. Now comes that challenging part! How does anyone begin to ascertain the level of happiness/unhappiness, satisfaction/dissatisfaction or fulfillment/unfulfillment in one's life? I remember visiting a poor Bahamian village where some of the homes still had earthen floors but the people seemed very content and quite happy. This, in sharp contrast to some of my acquaintances who live in pool-equipped mansions and drive luxury cars but don't appear to be nearly as happy — belying the "one who ends up with the most toys is the winner" philosophy. Alas, it *is* very difficult to quantify happiness but we need to do it in some manner unless we're willing to accept that . . . this is as good as it gets. If that is the case, fine — we've at least reached a conclusion we can feel good about. Next month's ***session with yourself*** will be different. Change *is* certain. Not one of us is the same person today as yesterday, nor will tomorrow's you be the same person you are today. Our bodies are constantly renewing themselves with new cellular growth making up for discarded molecules. Look at your fingernails. In less than five months they will be completely replaced. Each day the brain receives new data making for thousands of new synaptic connections. Indeed, very recent research indicates that even that wonderful organ replaces dying cells with new ones. *Nothing* stays the same.

You really *can't* swim in the same river twice. That's why it's so important to have regularly scheduled self-evaluations of how we are relating to our contextica. Not only are we constantly reconstructing, but the contexts we are in also transform — every second, every hour, every day of every year of our lives. A scheduled, formalized, personal, intellectual exploratory time is something many of us do each new year when we make an annual introspection and resolve to make perceived needed improvements in our lives. Comedians and cartoonists usually have a field day lampooning the process. ("This year I resolve <u>not</u> to make any more New Year's resolutions.") But the intent is praiseworthy and worth pursuing in a more structured and regular manner. Let's go through how a ***session with yourself*** might go.

This solitary and most personal self analysis — me in my hammock and you, wherever — begins with asking yourself the questions posed earlier in this section:

**Am I reasonably content, happy, satisfied, fulfilled:**

**. . . with my life in general?**
**. . . with relationships ( family, spouse, significant other, friends, co-workers)?**
**. . . with my job, education, avocation?**
**. . . with my physical condition?**

Now we're back to that puzzlement discussed earlier. How do I know if I'm reasonably happy, content, satisfied, fulfilled? This was the most vexing part of creating this book. It caused writer's block for several months. I researched everything I could find on the topic, looked at hundreds of self tests on just about every aspect of human behavior but could not come up with the right stuff. There are, indeed, many excellent and useful checklists or Likert-type scales (very unhappy, somewhat unhappy, neutral, somewhat happy, very happy), but they didn't quite lend themselves to ease of use for our purposes. Most seemed banal, complicated or too mechanical. Self-questioning formats seemed the most useful for our purposes of exploring various contexts of our lives. For our initial self-assessment we need only to simply ask ourselves two vital, important, crucial, pivotal, essential, compelling, profound and fundamental questions. The first:

### *Is this as good as it gets?*

If that splendid organ, your brain, signals "yes" — then count yourself most fortunate and go on to something else. You're all set until next month. But if you ask if this (my life in general, my job, my relationships, my financial situation, my health) is as good as it gets, and your answer is "no" or you're not sure — then we go on because, as we talked earlier, the grass *may very well be greener* on that other side of the fence. One of the worst admonitions ever given is "you made your bed, now you have to sleep in it." That's really absurd! The bed can be made differently or a new bed chosen if the present one is uncomfortable. In a free country other options are always there. One should never feel locked into a bad context.

**The grass may very well be greener on the other side of the fence.**

We need, then, to look at specific parts of our lives and to decide if there is a level of discontent sufficient to warrant considering a change to more verdant pastures or another bed. I told you this was the most challenging (read toughest) of the four steps. It's much easier in some areas than in others. Self-assessing your physical condition, as an example, could go: "no, my health is not as good as it (can) get . . . the charts and my doc tell me I'm twenty pounds too heavy . . . gotta lose some weight." Pretty clear cut, a discrete measurable situation. But if there is an uncertainty or "no" to the as-good-as-it-gets query when it's about, say, one's job, it's a much more complex undertaking involving many factors, most of which can only be subjectively evaluated. How big is the paycheck? What security do I have? Are the fringe benefits adequate? Are my talents being maximized? Do I get enough vacation time? Is my work fulfilling? Do I like the people I work with? How high can I go in this company or business? Am I happy in this job? While some of the answers to those questions can be objectively made (e.g., comparing my paycheck or fringe benefits with others in like positions is a matter of numbers) others can only subjectively be determined. Here we then have to turn to the second question:

### *Is there more pleasure or pain?*

The **pleasure/pain** psychological explanation of human behavior is really a very pertinent and most valuable way for us to explore subjective and highly personal areas. While Freud is most closely associated with the theory, many psychologists before and after have accepted its principles in various forms. For our purposes we'll simply state that it holds: humans are drawn to and will stay in situations, circumstances ( contextica) which give more pleasure than pain. Conversely, we tend to shy away from or leave those conditions which give more pain than pleasure. The terms "pleasure" and "pain" are, of course, interpreted very liberally to include:

**pleasure** as: bliss, happiness, joy, serenity, peace, well-being, contentment, gratification,satisfaction.

**pain** as: distress, discomfort, anguish, sadness, vexation, travail, remorse, boredom, unease.

Again — the two terms connote broad meanings beyond pleasure as "aaah," or pain as "ouch." Pleasure can range from the height of ecstasy to a simple feeling of tranquility while pain can include misery or extreme suffering to a light general feeling of unease. Using a scale/continuum for answering the question previously posed (as to whether one's work is more pleasureful or painful) with the midpoint representing pure neutral, we then come up with the best judgment we can in placing all the factors relating to our job on the line scale.

Jody Cantor works for a computer software company. Her pay is better than others in comparable positions and she gets excellent fringe benefits. Because of mergers and buyouts in the industry, she's a little uneasy about her job security and wonders if she is working below her ability. She gets along well with her superiors and her co-workers and also is optimistic about promotion to a higher position. Realizing that the factors she looked at are not equal in importance (a fat paycheck can make up for having to put up with boorish colleagues perhaps), but she can get a better impression as to whether or not to start thinking about a change in her employment. In Jody's case the "pleasure" of her job (good pay, excellent benefits, satisfaction with co-workers, etc.) outweighs the "pain" of concern about her job security. She'll stay where she is with perhaps a renewed appreciation for what she has and will look forward to vying for a promotion.

If Jody's conclusions about the factors she considered fell clearly on the right side of the scale/continuum, then the job is giving her more pain than pleasure and she should consider a change. As we'll see in future chapters, the process is not always that clear cut. Most of the time, the judgments will cluster around the midpoint of our scale/continuum making decisions hard to come by. The seesaw scale is then at a level position. When that happens it's better to wait for more time and information and not do anything — heeding the maxim: "when in doubt, do nothing." A tipping point may eventually be reached which will then spur action for a change.

A helpful variation of the scale/continuum is to use a simple pro and con sheet on which are listed all the favorable and positive factors in one column and all the unfavorable and negative aspects in an adjoining column. Putting thoughts down on paper or into a tape recorder gives order to the activity and also allows for some hitchhiking of ideas. Listing "good pay" may trigger consideration of "fringe benefits" as one example. "Have some seniority" may lead to concerns about the

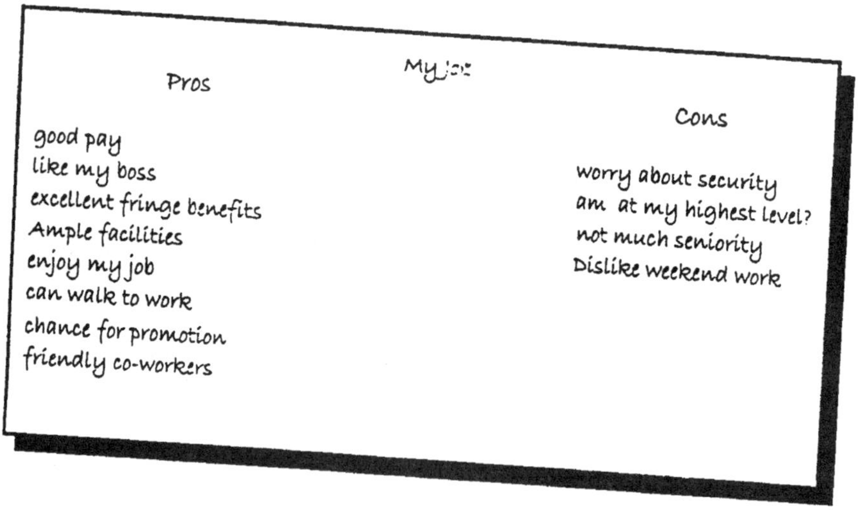

stability of the company in today's takeover climate of American business.

But the processes of using a scale/continuum or a pro/con listing can be carried out just mentally lying in a hammock or sunning on the beach. What's really important is to stand outside of yourself and give thought to your contextica in some regular and orderly manner. Unless we apply structure, thinking has a strong tendency to be unfocused, vague and easily distracted. Your mind will meander anywhere and everywhere, like a boat with a loose rudder, if you let it. We can visualize a scale/continuum or a pro/con sheet as we think about our self analysis, but, again, it's wise to then put it on paper as soon as one can . . . lest it be forgotten forever.

### The second step: Set Goals

Once you've determined where you are, then it becomes a question of where you want to go and that brings us to deciding on realistic, achievable and measurable objectives. It's somewhat difficult to formulate well-defined goals, but it is critically important that it be done — and done well — as it affects everything that follows. Setting the goal then mandates what course of action we will take and we don't want to go down the wrong road.

As an example, staying with the job area, let's assume that Jody Cantor's pleasure/pain continuum had everything weighted on the pleasure side with the single exception of her pay. She is happy with the fringe benefits, with her chances for promotion, has harmonious relations with her superiors and coworkers, experiences a high degree of satisfaction in her job, likes her time schedule and feels secure that the company will be in business a long time. She is having a tough time, however, making ends meet with the compensation she earns. The interest for her credit card balances is eating away at her disposable income. She is — as they say — living from paycheck to paycheck.

Understandably, Jody could come to what would seem to be an obvious goal: seek a higher-paying job. She has defined her problem unrealistically, setting an objective which may be entirely wrong for her. The problem may not be the size of her paycheck as much as it is the management of her finances, in which case a more appropriate goal would be to rid herself of debt and live within her income. To paraphrase the Biblical question: what does it profit a woman if she gains a fatter paycheck only to find herself in a place of work in which she is very unhappy? Goals must be realistic.

They should also be achievable. While it's O.K. to see the inspirational value of always striving for something just beyond reach, we should, however, set goals which can be reasonably attained within a certain time frame. Once a goal is set and then reached, another can be made for a different level. This is sensible near term and far term planning which greatly enhances the achievability of our objectives.

A high school classmate of mine has had a very successful practice of treating patients with severe obesity. Dr. Victor Vertes has helped hundreds of men and women lose significant poundage. His Cleveland, Ohio office has attracted people from all over the country who were afflicted with triple-digit overweightness. After a very thorough physical examination, the physician and patient would sit down together and set a realisitic long term final objective of reducing weight by, say, a hundred and twenty pounds *but* that goal was to be reached by a series of monthly steps of an amount of weight reduction considered safe by the doctor. Several near term achievements led to the successful accomplishment of a far term goal. Walking a mile *does* start with a first step and is completed by a succession of other steps.

**Think of a goal as a contract with yourself.**

In addition to being realistic and achievable, goals should be measurable. They should be stated in a manner which makes provision for evaluation. "I'm going to lose weight" may sound very commendable, but it lacks specificity as to how much and when. Think of a goal as a contract with yourself. A contract is legally worthless if it does not include express provisions as to the responsibilities of the parties involved and a definite time frame.

Finally, goals <u>must</u> be recorded. Write them down, talk them into your tape recorder, put them on your laptop or home computer . . . anywhere they'll get your regular attention. I hesitate to use the word "recorded" because it connotes the idea of storing information away in some file as in a county recorder's office. You want to be made regularly aware of your goals and that may involve posting them on the refrigerator under one of those nifty magnets or, for those computer wizards, creating a document which prompts an audio command of "You've got goals." (A <u>hitchhike</u> on AOL's famous line. ) But, whatever method you choose, the goal is to make sure you stay aware of your goals. (A quick digression . . . that last sentence reminds me of this.)

As an avid reader of the editorial pages of the local newspaper in the small resort town where I lived, the many letters of complaint caught my attention. Complaints ranged from heavy traffic because of the winter tourists to the water temperature of the swimming pools — too warm or too cold. It seemed people were always complaining about something. So I decided to send a letter to the editor in which I criticized the malcontents. It was only after I hit the "send" key launching the message irretrievably that I realized . . . *<u>I</u> was complaining about the complainers!*

Once you've determined areas of your life which need change and you have then set appropriate goals, you move forward to the action and fun part . . . **Self Starting** to attain those objectives creatively.

But, it's not always an easy task. So many things compete for your precious time. We talked about them earlier: the golf course, the 100 plus channels on television, surfing the web, etc., etc.

Yes it is tough to get started on a task, especially when it's as daunting as going into uncharted waters or perhaps addressing a problem which we hoped would just go away. All of our insecurities come into play. It is easy to ignore realities when all we have to do is click on the remote and our minds are immediately turned to viewing any of the scores of offerings on the magic tube. Remember our comment: "No two thoughts can occupy the brain at the same time." We have to really fight the temptation to allow *others* to control our precious minds.

Take a few minutes *now* and think about the last major decision you made. Was it about changing your job, buying or selling your house, getting married or divorced, purchasing a new automobile, or whatever? How long did it take you to reach a decision? Try to remember how much time elapsed between the first time you thought about it and when you ultimately acted. Did you put it off and if you did, what form did that procrastination take?

Before we go to the third step of our plan, let's keep in mind the wisdom of the fellow in this true fable (?) who sold a recalcitrant horse.

> The chaps in the town saloon were talking about the upcoming plowing season with one bragging about how his horse, Clementine, was the best, most hard-working and gentle animal he'd ever had. He went on and boasted that she could outwork a tractor and that she required very little feed. He was really sorry he had to sell her.

Another farmer, impressed with the description, offered to buy at the requested price.

When the new owner hitched Clementine to the plow, she wouldn't budge no matter how many "giddyaps" or pulls on the reins. Frustrated, he called the seller who immediately came over, took a two by four out of his truck and proceeded to strongly whack the mule on its hind whereupon it began to pull the plow. "You have to get her attention, first," he explained.

Weeks later the two were in the saloon and the new owner lamented: "She won't self-start, is lazy, eats a lot and needs to be beaten to work. She's a terrible critter!"

"Ya know," responded the former owner, "If you keep talking that way about the animal, you'll never sell her."

## The third step: *Self Start*

Yes, as we discussed in the section about potatoes, it is soooo easy to conform to that law (or is it a theory?) of physics which states that a body in motion tends to remain in motion and a body at rest tends to stay at rest. But if you've stayed with the book this far — and obviously you have or you wouldn't be reading this line — you're not gonna let that happen. You're ready to go!

This is the living action part of our four-step plan . . . where we start by setting up and then executing the things we need to do related to the goals arrived at from the first two steps. We've analyzed where we are, identified areas needing change, and we will now make those changes. Let's follow the previously-mentioned problem of weight control.

It seems that almost everyone in America is overweight and it's not just adults. The Surgeon-General of the United States issued a warning in the spring of 2002 that America's children were generally overweight and under exercised. Schools came under fire for cutting physical education classes while adding soft drink and candy vending machines. Although doctors are constantly reminding us that excess weight puts strain on the heart, increases blood pressure, adds stress on joints, makes breathing more difficult and, in general, shortens our life spans, we continue to largely ignore them while ordering that chocolate torte for dessert. Oh — we make some concessions. We buy anything that says it's "low fat" or "no fat." But how many times have you observed an obviously overweight person at a restaurant eating a huge meal but who has mustered the "will power" to wash it down with a diet Coke? Many Americans are killing themselves with forks.

So the goal of losing enough poundage to get within the suggested weight ranges would seem to be an appropriate one for many of us. (We're not *all* overweight. My cousin, Ethel, is a rail.) But let's say we set a goal of losing weight at the rate of five pounds a month (short term) for a (long term) total of thirty pounds. That's realistic, achievable and easily measurable. You are also going to record that, aren't you? Now what?

You decide on what you will do to reach the objective and then you do it. In making your personal plan of action you'll first look to conventional solutions or procedures which we'll call OT (orthodox thinking) and then . . . *and this is the most important message in this book* . . . you'll go on to apply CT (creative thinking). You will need to push your thinking to go beyond OT.The two, again, are not mutually exclusive but are to be viewed as being jointly valuable. The more methods used, the better are our decisions. The more we look, the more we'll see.

**Look at this . . . what do you see?**

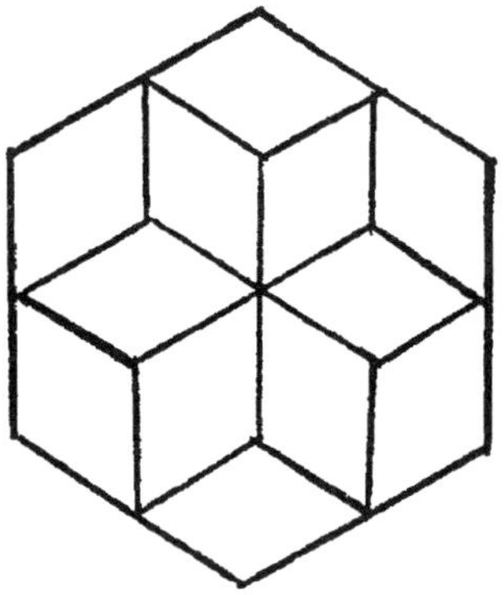

Is it a six-pointed star in a frame? Or do you see some cubes stacked as stairs, or, perhaps, the cubes are suspended from a corner of a ceiling? At first glance you'll see one of those configurations but if you take more time and focus on the drawing, you'll see the other two. If you concentrate long enough, I'm confident all three will appear. Keep staring.

The very important point is that we have to persevere; we have to push ourselves further. As in the nine-dots exercise, we should get into the habit of going beyond the obvious. There is *always* more than what initially meets the eye. The more you think, the more you'll discover. The usual reaction to a resolution to lose weight is: (1) cut down on food intake and (2) exercise more. Both are excellent solutions to the problem — much better than, say, buying larger clothes. They both lack specificity, however, as to how and when — exactly — this will be done. More to the point, though, is that this is a first flush . . . an initial and limited OT response. We need to apply the OT and the CT strategies described in Chapter III, Part 2. Getting started first involves deciding on the logical, the somewhat obvious ways (OT) of reaching our objectives — "rounding up the usual suspects" — so to speak. Elaborating on the two strategies of cutting down on food intake and exercising more by adding some specificity and then conscientiously implementing those strategies, will probably achieve what we want. But going further and using CT may elicit other, perhaps easier or more effective approaches.

Again, with the weight example, let's select CHECKLISTING from the CT techniques we reviewed in Chapter Three and apply it to our problem.

**Adapt . . . . . my garage or basement to a gymnasium.**
**. . . . . time schedule to accommodate more exercise.**

**Combine . . . trips to store, library, etc. with exercise by using bicycle instead of car.**
**. . . . . lunch hour with an exercise period.**

**Eliminate . . . one meal a day, cut out snacks and junk food.**

**Magnify . . . . commitment to achieve this goal.**
**Minify. . . . . . food portions.**
**Modify . . . . . my appetite by eating celery between meals.**

**Rearrange . . the refrigerator so all diet foods are in front.**
**Reverse . . . . dining sequence . . . eat dessert first, then less of the main dish.**

**Substitute . . 4% fat milk with skim milk.**

This is a rather limited listing but you get the idea. I'm sure you can add many more possibilities. CHECKLISTING is a great tool in helping us to explore beyond the obvious. It, and IDEATIONAL FLUENCY and FREE ASSOCIATION, can be used in just about any situation while the others, FORCED RELATIONSHIPS and MORPHOLOGICAL ANALYSIS, have more specialized applications.

The techniques all complement one another to some extent. FREE ASSOCIATION has us thinking about how many things (IDEATIONAL FLUENCY) we can come up with for the CHECKLISTING categories.

We want, then, to use all the resources we have to help attain our goals. Using OT *and* CT in concert will enable us to do just that.

### The fourth step: *Success*

So your *Self Analysis* led you to a *Set Goal* which you *Self Started* and have now completed. The last step is evaluating how you've done and then reveling in your *Success*! This is easy. You simply determine if you've achieved your objective. If you haven't, you can extend the time or develop a new goal.

But your realistic and easily measurable goal set six months ago of losing 30 pounds has been fully attained. Stepping on that scale shows a 32-pound reduction! Your doctor applauds, your wife and friends remark how great you look. You feel wonderful, haven't had that chronic heartburn and you now greet each morning with more vigor and enthusiasm. Indeed . . . how sweet it is!

Would this have been accomplished without the four-step or some other plan? Most probably not. I remember well the remarks of one of the participants in a graduate seminar on creativity held some years ago at the University of California at Davis. We were brainstorming about how to impress students with the importance of planning. He gave the example of going from point "A" to point "B" in a ship or a plane. Getting to the destination (goal) involves setting a course along one of the 360 degrees of the compass. If we fail to plan the correct one, the chances are **359 to 1** against our getting to where we want to go. Why buck those odds? It *is* true . . . if you don't know where you're going, any road will get you nowhere.

In the remaining chapters, we'll present a miscellany of examples, research, insights, techniques and methods you can use to examine in greater detail how creative contexting can be helpful in the areas of: schooling and work, relationships, use of time, and money matters.. Finally we'll summarize the major points of our journey and close with a miscellany of related topics. Let's proceed after this humor break which reminds us that change is inexorably certain and inescapably constant. Buddha's last words were: "All things of this world are subject to constant change. Be mindful and strive on." It's true . . . not one of us is the same person we were yesterday."

In case you didn't see all three versions of the figure a few pages back, this may help.

six-pointed star

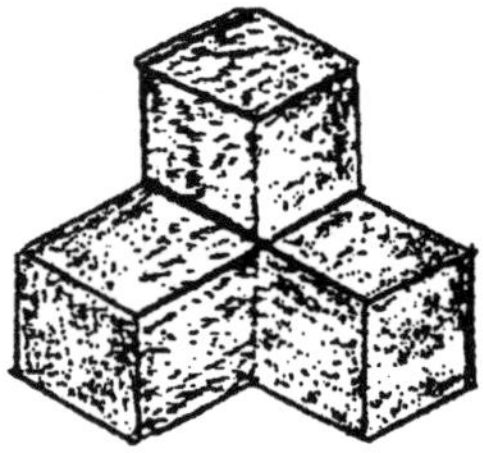

cubes as stairs

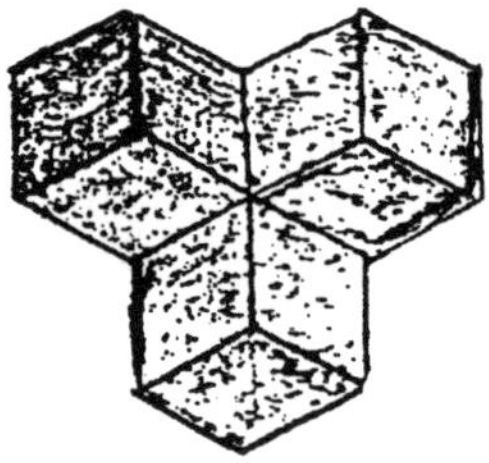

cubes suspended from ceiling

Chapter Six

# CONTEXTICA: EARLY YEARS, SCHOOLING AND WORK

***"Think of your transfer this way Fenton. Here you're a small potato. In our Hicksville office, you'll be the big kahuna."***

In our lifetimes during infancy and childhood, decisions are made for us by others with responsibility for our well being. Beginning at birth, our parents must decide if we're to be born at home or in a hospital, by the Lamaze or Boyer method, with or without the husband present. They also have the option of knowing, before the delivery, if the newcomer is a boy or a girl so that the nursery can be appointed in the appropriate decor. (Is it still blue for boys and pink for girls?) At the end of this earthly experience, our final context is also determined by others — although we may have had input as to our wishes — as to whether there will be cremation or burial or perhaps the body will be given over for organ transplants or medical training. There is also an option of cryonics where the body is frozen until some future date when it will be thawed to a hoped-for new life. We now even have the choice of having our remains sent out to the space heavens. A company in California (where else) will rocket your ashes to the moon for a mere $12,500.

Between birth and death, major and minor contextual decisions confront us every day. Where shall I eat lunch today? Where should I take my wife dining tonight? What school should I choose? Is it time to change where I live or work? When should I ask the boss for a raise? Where and when should we vacation this year? Should I retire to Florida, Arizona, or California? When is the best time to buy that house or business?

Most people make the minor contextical decisions almost automatically, through habit or convenience. Lunch is at Ron's Pub because it's only minutes from the office and I've always eaten there. I also eat at the designated lunch hour even though I bitch about the crowd and the wait.

### *The Schooling Years*

Major contextical decisions are largely made for us by our parents until we near maturity and have to begin to determine the courses of our lives. Important choices begin occurring in the middle and senior high school years when we start consciously selecting friends, joining clubs, and getting involved in athletics and other extracurricular activities. The selection of courses — which may or may not have parental input — starts to shape our socioeconomic futures; we get tracked as college preparatory, vocational-technical, or general. After graduation, the contexts we choose become very crucial. Off to a public or private college or some other school? Take a job? Join the armed services? Get married?

Formal or informal contexting pervades our society's schools and colleges. At the elementary level, for instance, pupils are often grouped with others of similar abilities and learning rates. In a typical first-grade classroom, there will usually be the three reading groups: the "Robins" (fast), the "Bluebirds" (average), and the "Sparrows" (slower). Before first-grade, parents face several important contextical decisions, such as whether or not to enroll their children in preschool programs. What kind of program? Permissive Montessori, rigidly disciplined, religious are among the options. Enrolling the child in a public or private school poses another extremely important question as to the *when.* If a child beginning school is on the young side of her chronological age group, she may have to struggle all through the thirteen years of education, and even beyond, competing with others who are a full year older. As an elementary school principal for many years, I would always counsel parents — of the younger-in-their-age-group of prospective kindergartners — to give their children the advantage of being on the older side of their class. The added maturity would be significant in their academic pursuits. In other areas of the school experience, we can easily appreciate the advantage the seventeen-year-old quarterback, cheerleader, starting pitcher prospect has over his or her sixteen-year-old classmates.

With the current national emphasis on minimum standards, accountability, and achievement test criteria — the case for later enrollment is even more compelling. When I was principal of a large elementary school in Sarasota County (Florida) back when the accountability fervor began, we "flunked" *one of every four pupils* before they reached the second grade! This get-tough retention policy has now become typical for most school districts and will result in much larger percentages as the opposition to social promotions mounts — which is happening now. Many educators attribute the youngsters' failures to immaturity for the grade level. We conducted some research and did indeed find that a disproportionate number of the youngsters who had to do the year over were on the young side, chronologically. I am absolutely sure in my mind that, for many of those children, better educational contexting — placing them in the right group at the right time — would have avoided having them judged as "failures" so early in their educational careers. In the middle and high school years, students (and parents) face very important choices regarding course selection. They may select chemistry, physics and advanced mathematics while others go with less demanding offerings which then narrows their post-high-school options.

In some senior high schools, students are classified into formal achievement/ability tracks. In Shaker Heights, Ohio, public schools use a levels program. Level IV is for the college-bound while Level I is for those who will probably not go on to post-high-school academic pursuits. Although counselors play a major role in determining if a student can be successful at a certain level, any student may request — and be granted — any level placement.

This is contextical decision-making in its purest form. At that crucial juncture in life, a student will be placing himself in the company of future engineers, doctors, lawyers, scientists — or, would-be mechanics, secretaries, nurses or sales clerks. Let me be quick to say that no value judgement is intended in the differentiation of these vocations — a good mechanic is of more value to society than a bad doctor — but the point is that the context (group, level, class or school) one is in will almost surely dictate the future. The levels program at Shaker Heights has been highly acclaimed nationally. The school is a consistent leader in the number of National Merit Scholars and has been honored as one of the ten best senior highs in the country. The program has its drawbacks, however. Students may choose lower-level subjects because of laziness or lack of confidence or poor counseling. An unrealistic choice can result in frustration and embarrassment when the student can't cope with advanced material. Tracking or grouping of any kind has always been controversial in American public education. Egalitarians have passionately charged that such academic programs are elitist and, therefore, undemocratic.

**The school context one is in will almost surely dictate the future.**

### *Our Jock Mentality*

There doesn't seem to be much concern, however, for the unabashed elitism of all of our high schools when it comes to sports. If you consider the salaries of coaches, large costs of stadiums, equipment and supplies, the honors (banquets, trophies and publicity) and special treatment for athletes — it must be admitted that we are certainly guilty of creating an elite group in just about all our high school societies. Let me hasten to add that there is much value in school varsity programs. I credit varsity sports with keeping me, and countless others, in school. School spirit engendered by enthusiasm for the "Fighting Eagles," the "Hawks," the "Lions" or some other team moniker is an important part of the high school journey. But I deplore the emphasis we place on a few students when it's at the expense of the larger student body and the academic program. A tragic aspect of this was seen in the Columbine (Colorado) high school calamity of 1998, when two students gunned down several of their classmates in a rage against the school's athletes.

The area of sports provides us with another example of deliberate contexting. "Seeding" is widely practiced to ensure that the better athletes are not eliminated too early in tournaments. In tennis, a Martina Hingis and a Venus Williams will rarely oppose each other until the semifinal or final rounds. Without this contexting, the top talents might be defeated in the early stages; the final contest could well be an awful mismatch as a result.

Contexting is also practiced in the different leagues or levels of competition set up by high school, college and professional associations. State high school athletic associations have their triple A, four A and five A categories. Colleges have their conferences and professional baseball has its major and minor leagues. Time contexting in collegiate sports is practiced in "redshirting" — the policy of holding back freshman athletes to gain the maximum effectiveness of the player during a limited eligibility period.

Where to attend college certainly brings up many questions for the creative contexter. Go to a big or small, one near home or away, private or state? According to annual surveys done by the National Association of State Universities, tuition costs for private colleges are two and three times higher than for a public institution. Although accepted by a top-rated, prestigious law school, a friend's son opted for a second tier university because he felt his chances of making law review would be much better (and <u>much</u> cheaper) at the lesser rated school. The “small frog in the big pond” factor, money and scholarship possibilities, comparative costs-of-living in different cities, climate, distance to home are all things to consider. John McPherson’s cartoon presents yet another (we hope not) important factor in making a choice:

Reprinted with permission of UNIVERSAL PRESS SYNDICATE

. . . but if this is a high priority for some, there are at least two magazines who do annual pieces on “best party colleges.”

### *Tote That Barge . . . Lift That Bale"*

In the new millennium we Americans are spending more and more of our time in the workplace. Our average work week is now 47 hours — up from 43 in just the last 20 years. We work about *eight weeks* longer, on average per year, than our European counterparts! We've even surpassed the Japanese who are taking it a little easier. And of all modern industrialized societies, the International Labor Organization's statistics for 1998 show the Norwegians working only 1339 hours per year which comes out to a lean *27 hour* work week! That's 57% of our weekly regimen. Obviously, Norwegians have much more time for leisure activities, creative thinking, time with their families and friends, etc. When is the next plane to the land of the Vikings?

Now I know you're not going to be booking the next flight to Europe because you can work much fewer hours there for the same (or, some would say, a better) standard of living. But the "where" of our job is a very important factor that should deserve a lot more of our attention. In today's corporate world, advancing to a higher and more lucrative position is often tied to relocating to another city. Let's look at a couple of examples of how our work location affects our pocketbooks or wallets.

### *The Tale of Two Lawyers*

Jeff Benson and Roger Lattimore both work for the same law firm at identical salaries in one of downtown Denver's high-rise buildings — the one nicknamed "the mailbox" because of its striking resemblance to those letter drops — and both commute to work. Jeff bought a remodeled house in a rejuvenated neighborhood just outside the downtown area — about three miles from his office. Roger purchased a home in the suburb of Broomfield — some 33 miles away. On average, it takes Jeff about 10 minutes to drive to work while Roger needs three-quarters of an hour. Jeff's and Roger's Corollas each average approximately 30 miles per gallon of gas.

So each workday that the young lawyers go to fight the legal wars, Roger spends an hour more driving (going and returning) and burns two gallons more of gasoline than Jeff. Over a 240-day work year, Jeff gains the equivalent of 30 eight-hour days to do whatever else he wishes. You might say he has well over a month's vacation time than his colleague. And figuring the cost of gasoline at, say, a buck and a quarter a gallon — Roger is six hundred dollars poorer than his co-worker. The Hertz Corporation computes annual costs of driving (which include insurance, depreciation, maintenance, etc.) at $.50 per mile which would then bring Roger's annual cost of getting to and from work to a whopping $7200 compared to Jeff's of $720 — *a tenfold* difference! Jeff, in effect, makes almost $6500 a year more for doing the same work at the same place. Also he devotes *a month less* of his time to the firm than his cohort.

In a full page ad, Marriott Town Residences in Miami touts "*43 extra days a year to live*" if you reside in one of their close-in condominiums and your place of employment is near their complex.

Of course, there are many other considerations in deciding where one should live besides nearness to the work place. Millions reside great distances from their offices or shops tolerating the daily, long commutes with the additional time and expense involved because they value a suburban or exurban setting. They're willing to spend the subsequent time and money in a quest for a safer neighborhood, more space or better schools. Some even cherish the additional travel hours as time for relaxation or meditation, though they may have other feelings on days of traffic tieups due to weather or accidents.

It becomes, then, a matter of "to each his own." Relating the pleasure/pain continuum or a pro/con sheet to the two lawyers' decisions to live where they do, would reflect the importance each places on: money, time, safety, convenience, schools, nearness to relatives and friends, and a myriad of other possible factors. Safety, in Roger's thinking, may have to do with crime rates as between cities and environs: Jeff may interpret safety more with statistics that show he is four times less likely to be involved in a traffic accident because of his shorter time on the highways. Indeed — "one man's meat is another man's indigestion" . . . or something like that.

Incidentally, the building where I met Jeff and Roger — "the mailbox" — has an interesting story relating to an initial poor context decision. Apparently, the 32-story edifice with its eye-catching hooded top was originally designed to be built in Houston, Texas. It was, however, put up in downtown Denver. The first winter's snowfall accumulated heavily on its sloped rooftop. When a shining sun melted the snow, Denverites — on streets on one side of the structure as motorists or pedestrians — got an unanticipated white avalanche and a later waterfall as Mother Nature did her thing. The problem has since been resolved.

I used the term "tale" in describing the different contexts of the two lawyers in Denver which may be interpreted as being a fictional account. Not so. It really happened just as this ensuing story of two educators is factual, not fictional.

### *Case Study: Two Teachers*

Two women — graduated 30 years ago from Kent State University's (Ohio) school of education — accepted positions as primary grade teachers: one in a suburban Cleveland district, the other in a rural school in the western part of Ohio. Both retired last year. They taught the same grades of essentially middle-class pupils and each went on to attain master's degrees and tenure in their respective districts. Karen's starting annual salary in the Shaker Heights (Ohio) School District was $6400. while Marie earned $6000.for her first year in the Fostoria City School District. Because Karen worked in one of the highest paying districts, there was a $400. difference between her salary and that of Marie's, who contracted with one of the lowest paying districts in the state. That differential remained approximately the same throughout their teaching careers resulting in Marie's total compensation for the thirty years coming out to $12,000. *less* than her former college classmate's!

Ohio's teacher retirement system computes annual pension amounts by multiplying a teacher's final average (the best of the last three years) salary by the number of — years of service multiplied by two. Confusing? Karen's final average salary was $60,400. (Both teachers worked for 30 years.) Multiplying 30 times two, she receives 60% of her final average salary for the rest of her life, which works out to an annual retirement of $36,264. Under the same formula, Marie, who finished teaching with a final average of $56,200. will receive $33,720. per year. Both retired at age 52. Assuming the current life expectancy of women to be 78 years, during their retirement years, Karen will gain $66,144. *more* than Marie should they both conform to the actuary's time table of when the grim reaper will arrive.

So here we have two professionals — with the same education, having done essentially the same work, for the identical number of years — whose variation in salary remuneration was $12,000. and whose estimated retirement benefits difference will be $66,144. *for a grand total of $78,144!*

Again, as with the two lawyers, money certainly isn't the sole consideration in determining where one will work — but it is important. Marie chose to teach in Fostoria because that was her home while Karen, who also came from a small Ohio town, opted to work where she would get the better paycheck. The same wide disparities within a state in teacher — or police, fire, and other government employees for that matter — salaries are also evident among states. Employees and retired workers from New Jersey, New York, Minnesota, Michigan, and California fare much better financially than those toiling in South Dakota, Mississippi, Alabama and Florida. This generally holds true for the private as well as the public sector. A carpenter, electrician — or a teacher — in Florida is paid significantly less than their counterparts in most northern areas.

Convicted thief Willie Sutton, when asked why he robbed banks, replied — "because that's where the money is." When choosing where you will work, why *not* consider where in your locality, state or anywhere in the nation you can get the most money. In today's mobile society the typical worker changes jobs seven times in a lifetime. Thirty-six of every 100 American men change jobs each year. Twenty-six out of every 100 women do that. We are free to live and work wherever we please in this great nation. There are no gates or "checkpoint Charlies" at any of our states' borders. Why not go where the best opportunities are? Many, of course, are doing just that — creating the satellite families now so common. Although I lamented about it in a preceding chapter (my son in Australia, daughter in Japan, etc.), I realize they must go where challenges beckon. The wonderful cyberworld of e-mail capability and speedy jet air travel mitigate, somewhat, the distances among us.

While money is a major factor in deciding our school and workplace choices, another is the level of achievement one may aspire to. If you want to go to the top of certain professions, you have to go where the action is. Computer whizzes flock to Silicon Valley, aspiring actors gravitate to Hollywood, while vintners will find — not only the right soil — but also association with people of similar interests in California's Napa Valley. Going over to the other coast, New York City is still the major Mecca for the most prestigious publishers, advertising agencies and models. "If you can make it there . . . you'll make it anywhere" is the song's famous melodic commendation of America's great metropolis.

### *The Golden Years*

And when our careers are near completion and we prepare for retirement, the quest for the best place and the most propitious time begins. Go to Florida, Arizona, Texas, California or stay where we are? Take early retirement or work longer?

Most retirees have to adjust to a fairly fixed income so the purchasing power of their pension checks becomes very significant. They also tend to feel secure in their present settings where there are familiar faces. But here's a beyond-the-nine-dots choice my favorite barber of many years made.

Bela (Bill) Lang left Hungary for the United States when he was eighteen. Shortly after his arrival his draft number came up on the same day as ex-president William Clinton's. Bela served three years in the army and then settled in the Cleveland area where for 30 years he worked as a barber who rose to the ownership of three tonsorial parlors. He visited his homeland often — having dual citizenship in the U.S. and Hungary — and married a woman from a village near his birthplace during a recent visit.

Although Bela loves this country and is proud of his military service and what he has achieved here with his businesses, he is planning to sell his shops, cars and his house and retire to Hungary next year. When I asked why, he replied that part of the reasoning was that his wife and he had relatives there but the major attraction was financial. Here, in retirement, he would be comfortable — money wise — by U.S. standards, but in Hungary he could "live like a king!" There, they could live in a mansion, have domestic help for one-fourth of what it would cost in the states, could travel in high style and dine in the very best restaurants. In Hungary *they* would be the "Joneses" as in "keeping up with the Joneses." *They* would be the big frogs in the smaller pond.

Millions of Americans elect to retire in other countries where their dollars will buy a lot more creature comforts than would be the case here. In Mexico's San Miguel de Allende, one-third of the population is American. As many as 30,000 U.S. citizens are said to live in Guadalajara, the second largest city, and there is a sizable colony in sun-splashed Cuernavaca. The consul for that region distributes over 24,000 monthly Social Security and government retirement checks which then buy many weak pesos for a strong dollar. There — like Bela in Hungary — one can afford servants and amenities which may be out of reach at home.

Costa Rica has also been a favorite place for an estimated 30,000 yankee retirees who enjoy living in central America's "Switzerland" — that peace-loving democracy which maintains no military forces. With its mountains, seashores and tropical breezes — it's a nearer and cheaper Hawaii.

The State Department estimates that of all of us living abroad, about one-third are in Europe (mostly in the United Kingdom, West Germany and Italy). There is also a sizable number of us living in the islands of the Caribbean which fly the star-spangled banner — St. Croix, St. Thomas, Puerto Rico. The inspiration for moving to those places may not be monetary as much as it is a desire for adventure or new experiences in different cultural settings. Or, perhaps there is a yearning for a return to roots in the land of one's ancestors. It's a good idea to consider trying out an area before making too great a commitment. An extended visit, possibly for a year to experience all the seasonal changes, will help insure that it's a suitable choice. Check into the possibility of renting your home to defray some if not all of the expense of the relocation. There are organizations which match families in different regions who are willing to swap homes for a given period. Barbara and Lou Krane exchanged their Boca Raton condominium for a small villa in Ireland for a year and were ecstatic about the experience, although they decided against retiring to the Emerald Isle. Temporary changes in context such as that (they're now looking into a six-month swap with a family in Buenos Aires) can be very stimulating and enjoyable.

Whatever the reason, the decision as to the "where" of our golden years presents an exceptionally important contextical challenge. The "golden years" are much too valuable to be marred by hasty actions which could result in a really bad choice.

Applying some of our creative thinking techniques to this matter, we could use CHECKLISTING, DAYDREAMING, and/or MORPHOLOGICAL ANALYSIS.

CHECKLISTING should be a first step. With the help of your partner, friends and relatives, the local library and your computer — all the possibilities can be listed. After putting down the obvious places, go beyond the nine dots and list some "far out" locations. Brainstorm to as many as you can without regard as to their feasibility. The best idea comes from a lot of ideas.

Just musing about those different places where you might like to live can be most helpful. DAYDREAMING about living in the mountains of the Carolinas or in the tropics of Hawaii or Florida or in a different country can give one a virtual feel of what the actual experience may be. You don't need to buy a ticket or get hotel reservations . . . you just go there immediately — free!

Finally, set up a two-dimensional matrix to start to align your dreams with reality. On the horizontal plane would be listed all the locations pared down from the results of your listing. On the other would be all the factors you consider important. This MORPHOLOGICAL ANALYSIS might look like this:

***Where to Retire . . . Lou and Barbara Krane***

| | *stay home* | *Florida* | *Arizona* | *California* | *Europe* | *Costa Rica* | *Mexico* |
|---|---|---|---|---|---|---|---|
| *safety* | 9 | 9 | 9 | 9 | 5 | 3 | 2 |
| *near kids* | 6 | 6 | 5 | 5 | 1 | 1 | 1 |
| *climate* | 4 | 10 | 8 | 7 | 4 | 10 | 9 |
| *cultural* | 10 | 8 | 5 | 8 | 9 | 5 | 5 |
| *housing* | 2 | 8 | 5 | 3 | 9 | 9 | 9 |
| *taxes* | 1 | 10 | 6 | 1 | 5 | 5 | 5 |
| *cost, living* | 3 | 9 | 5 | 2 | 5 | 9 | 9 |
| *recreation* | 6 | 9 | 10 | 5 | 7 | 8 | 5 |
| *ambience* | 10 | 10 | 8 | 5 | 10 | 5 | 5 |
| *church* | 10 | 9 | 5 | 5 | 5 | 5 | 5 |
| *medical* | 10 | 10 | 9 | 9 | 5 | 3 | 1 |
| *Totals* | 71 | 98 | 75 | 59 | 65 | 63 | 56 |

And the winner is . . . ! Clearly Florida emerged as the choice of Barbara and Lou. Together they talked about the factors which they considered important and assigned a number with “10" being the most favorable and “1" the least. When they were undecided, they would give a neutral “5" to the cell.

Safety had a high priority with them. They gave high marks to their own location and also figured they’d be O.K. in one of Florida’s, Arizona’s or California’s gated communities. They weren’t so sure of Europe and had some concern about Costa Rica and Mexico.

Nearness to their children was very important but just one of their offspring still resided in the Scarsdale area. The other two were in Washington, D.C. They reasoned that the kids could fly to them for vacations in Florida much easier than to the other locations under consideration.

They rated housing in the “stay at home” column a “2" because they owned a five-bedroom, four-bath residence which, needed through the child raising years, was now much too large for them. Besides, selling the place would net a large amount of money (they bought it for a song and could sell it like a symphony) which would easily pay for a smaller place in Florida and moving expenses with enough left over to substantially enhance their investment portfolio. This, partly due to the change in tax regulations which significantly benefits those who sell a personal residence.

Looking at one more line, the Kranes wanted to be near good medical facilities. Lou was beginning to experience some discomfiture in an arthritic hip and Barbara had high blood pressure. They were satisfied that the area they were considering in Florida had excellent doctors and hospitals nearby which would meet their particular health needs. Of course, people with certain conditions such as asthma or allergies must be especially cautious in their choice of where to live. If I had a serious heart condition — where immediate attention to an attack could mean the difference between life and death — Seattle, Washington would merit consideration. That city is consistently rated tops in response time of medical emergency mobile units. With the increasing presence of the personal cell phone it would be heartening (some kind of pun *is* intended here) to know that in the event of a coronary, help is quickly available . . . average response time: 3.3 minutes.

The Kranes made the final decision together knowing that *both* had to agree on the outcome of the process. It would have been a mistake to have done otherwise . . . with one partner being happy and the other . . . miserable.

The use of the matrix provides a systematic and intelligent way of helping to make an important decision provided full attention is given to the proper weight of the different factors.

Does living in sunshine outweigh nearness to long time friends? Again . . . to each his own.

### ***When to Retire***

Bill Vorlicky was an assistant superintendent in the Bedford, Ohio, school district having worked there in various positions for 45 years. Well liked by just about everybody — students, teachers, parents, other administrators — he relished going to his office each day. He could have retired 15 years earlier but he continued to work despite the fact that he was earning *just ten cents of a dollar*.

Remember Ohio's retirement formula of multiplying years of service by two which, in his case, meant he'd get 90% of his salary if he stayed home? He had to have loved his job. From a strict financial point of view, he could have started drawing his pension and taken another full or part-time position and been much richer.

Captain Bernard Silk took early retirement from the United States Marine Corps (20 years service, half pay) and opened a string of pizza stores in Ft. Lauderdale. With his service pension as a base, he and his wife ventured into a business in which they had no experience but were able to achieve great success . . . as defined by owning a mansion and boat on the intracoastal waterway.

The educator and the marine-turned-entrepreneur illustrate how subjective the decision, as to when to retire, is. Adding to the dilemma is the current practice of many employers to offer large bonuses for early retirement. Replacing a worker at the top of the salary schedule with a newcomer at the bottom is very cost-effective in some organizations. The potential retiree in the Social Security system has to decide whether to start benefits at age 62 or 65. Working the additional three years means a bigger check for life. Opting for the earlier age may enable the pursuit of other interests — travel, hobbies, starting a business, etc. — while one is younger and still enthusiastic.

**Retiring earlier may allow for the pursuit of other interests while one is younger and more enthusiastic.**

On a personal note, I retired from my professional career at age 52 and, since I was also eligible for Social Security benefits, I took those at age 62. Both were the earliest possible times and the choices were largely influenced by Harry Berman and Murray Schneider.

Harry owned an electronics retail store and Murray was a professor at Case-Western Reserve University. Both died at age 50 — Harry while lifting weights at the YMCA and Murray during his daily three-mile jog. Their premature deaths have always been reminders to me that the future is *never* guaranteed; that "nothing is certain . . . not even that nothing is certain." Now, *really* is the best of times. All right, enough platitudes already. You get my point.

* * * *

In this chapter we've reviewed the importance of choosing the right contextica in some aspects of our lives: parenting, childhood, education, work and retirement. Examples were given in using some creativity techniques to help make the best decisions.

Let's now go on to the enormous importance of contextica to our relationships.

But before we go on . . . Let's take this page as a break to think about our own personal experiences in our early childhood, schooling and work and reflect a bit on when we were in right places and right times and are now glad of it.

On the other hand, recall those times when you've been in clearly wrong places and ask "Why"?

## Chapter Seven

# CONTEXTICA: RELATIONSHIPS

### *Friends*

(Reprinted with special Permission of King Features Syndicate.)

Chris Browne's hilarious cartoon says it all. Our circles of friends determine to a very large measure who we are. You *do* become for better or worse — given enough time — like the people with whom you associate. Penologists constantly proclaim the dangers of putting young or first-time offenders into penitentiaries with hardened criminals. We know that criminal societies breed new criminals. Denzel Washington, the Oscar-winning actor, credits his mother's decision — to place him in a Catholic private school — for his success. She was concerned that the public school he would have attended might be a place of gang influence and a lack of discipline. Robert Vaughn, after achieving success in motion pictures and television, decided to move his family to Connecticut from California so that his children could attend schools which did not have the glitz and glamour and possibly spoiling influence of a Hollywood High.

Friendships are determined in childhood and in the growing years by the contexts we're in: the neighborhood, day care centers, schools and churches. As we progress into the middle and high school years, selectivity comes into play. We begin to choose from a larger pool those with whom we associate. In high school and college, we may enter into a very formalized contextual choices for making friends by joining a sports team, interest group, sorority, fraternity, club or society.

During the work years, friendships may continue from those earlier times or they may fall by the wayside. New associations then come from the work place, changed neighborhoods and churches, friends of spouses, friends of friends, clubs or random meetings.

We ought to choose our context of friends very carefully. One of the great blessings of life is enjoying the company of people we like to be with, whom we trust and can depend on. Friendships also pose an obligation on both parties to constantly nurture the relationship . . . never taking it for granted.

On the other hand, we should avoid, and never hesitate to end, relationships which are unpleasant or harmful. Stay well away from people who criticize or tear you down or are consistently negative. Who needs 'em? Life really is too short to suffer fools as friends. Your periodic *session with yourself* should include an appraisal of all your friendships. Strive to maintain and enhance those which are fulfilling, pleasant and mutually beneficial and

**Life is really too short to suffer fools as friends.**

end those which are negative, harmful or dangerous. Applying the pleasure/pain technique can help guide us as to our choices of friends. As in this example, information drawn from experiences leads to a "tipping point" in which there is finally an exclamation of "I've had it!"

Heather Jackson, my student intern, had been close with Dawn ever since they were classmates in elementary school. After confiding with me as to her increasing problems with Dawn, she decided to end the long relationship citing all the reasons why. Given her longstanding friendship with Dawn, it was not an easy decision.

Applying one creative approach, the pleasure/pain illustration for her situation would look like this:

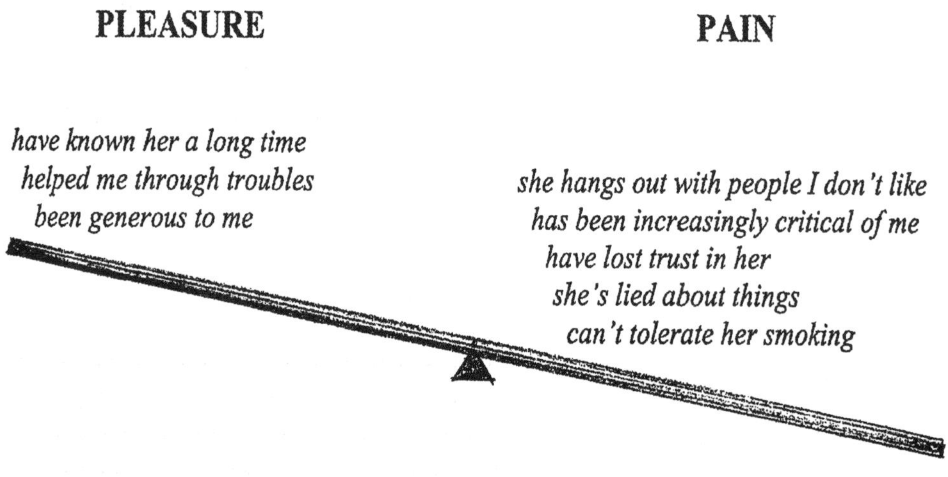


Again, a subjective decision as to the relative importance or weight of each item is necessary. Heather was deeply concerned about Dawn's drug involvement and that was a very strong tipping point factor for her — far outweighing the other considerations. Heather tried on many occasions to talk to Dawn about the dangers of the drug scene but to no avail. Discussions turned into heated arguments. She could no longer socialize with her friend without the presence of Dawn's new cohorts and that was unacceptable to her. Sadly, but necessarily, it was time to end that friendship.

Yes . . . friends are blessings but they can also be curses as Gary Hart, Bill Clinton, Patricia Hearst, Julius Caesar and a host of others would probably testify. Choose them as if your (quality of) life depended on them . . . *it does.*

### *Lovers*

If sex isn't the most intense and pleasurable activity of humankind (and other kinds as well), it's certainly in the top five. Not since Biblical times — when women were stoned to death for alleged sexual transgressions — has it been so hazardous to make physical love. It's now more crucial than ever that we choose the right contexts for this area of our lives.

Today, lovers face the risk of several new sexually-transmitted diseases in addition to the older ones of syphilis and gonorrhea. Chlamydia (a form of gonorrhea which persists despite penicillin treatment), herpes simplex and AIDS, pose real dangers. At this writing there is no cure for herpes or AIDS — and the latter has an eventual 100% mortality rate. AIDS, once thought to be associated only with homosexual relations and contaminated drug needles, is now found extensively in the general population as

**Choose your friends as if the quality of your life depended on them. It does.**

well. One shudders at the growing odds of encountering someone with these afflictions, especially since a prospective sex partner may be a carrier without knowing about it or showing any obvious symptoms.

**Not since Biblical times has it been so hazardous to make physical love.**

The diseases are increasing dramatically, here and elsewhere. AIDS has reached epidemic proportions in most sub-Saharan African countries including its alleged birthplace, Zaire. The far east is also experiencing significant numbers of AIDS cases. China, where the disease was unheard of a few years ago, is now concerned that it may reach an epidemic level. Closer to home, AIDS has become a major killer of men between 15 and 50 in New York City and San Francisco.

Even before the deaths of Rock Hudson and Arthur Ashe focused attention on the disease, our mores were changing as a defensive reaction to the new social maladies. The institution of marriage (or quasi-marriages — as in significant relationships) regained popularity because a monogamous union gave greater security that a sexual partner would be disease-free. (Not complete security, of course; adultery and philandering are by no means extinct.)

A new body of law relating to sexual behavior is emerging. If one gets a sexually-transmitted disease, can the transmitter be successfully sued for not informing the victim beforehand? If the disease is AIDS, could the transmitter be guilty of murder? Probably a moot point since that person is, perhaps, already under a death sentence.

It, then, behooves us to know more about our love-partner contexts. "Getting to know you" was pleasant to hear in *The King and I* but has a world of new meaning for us now. Since celibacy is not a viable option for most of us — human nature being what it is — it's crucial that we be more communicative and observant before we get orgasmic. It really could be a matter of life or death.

Finding out more about a person's lifestyle, frankly discussing concerns about disease, observing for symptoms, using condoms, and thorough pre- and post-coital showering are all in order today. Hey . . . here comes another great cliche: "better to be safe than sorry."

On a more positive note, let's turn to the subject of when and where potential love partners meet. We've seen how Mitzi Ross creatively picked the right time and the right place to meet her husband. What are some other creative ways?

### *Where the Boys/Girls Are*

Books, magazines, talk shows all provide advice on using creative social contexting to find a companion or mate. There's a plethora of advice on how to meet that man for every woman and vice versa. Most urge the reader to get out of the house and seek those contexts where prospective mates may be. From a review of scores of publications and several radio and television talk show programs, the following list emerges which includes the usual (within the nine dots) opportunities as well as many creative possibilities to meet Ms. or Mr. Wonderful.

Relating to our creative strategies, this CHECKLIST could come as a result of IDEATIONAL FLUENCY based on some researching just reviewed in the last paragraph. FREE ASSOCIATION could enlarge the list and then FORCED RELATIONSHIPS or a MORPHOLOGICAL ANALYSIS could then be applied.

## WHERE TO MEET HER OR HIM

**visit libraries, video stores**

**go to singles bars, coffee houses**

**attend horse races**

**go to polo matches**

**check out the people at workplace, school, college**

**get a part-time job**

**take adult education, life guarding, martial arts courses**

**go to car races, museums, auto and boat shows**

**run at the local high school track**

**participate in bowling, bicycling, hiking, fishing, tennis, racquetball activities**

**enroll in computer camps**

**shop grocery supermarkets**

**attend investment seminars**

**go on a cruise**

**join a hostel travel group**

**enlist in the armed forces**

**join the Peace Corps**

**move to another city or country**

**use a dating service**

### *Singles Bar Contexts*

> **Bars reflect the classes of the larger society.**

Night clubs, lounges, single bars are great places to meet potential partners in spite of the bad rap they get as "meat markets" and their negative reputation from the movie *Looking for Mr. Goodbar*. They're not all loaded with weirdos. Of course, one should be cautious wherever one goes. There are over 35,000 singles bars in the nation and they can be categorized contextually. The "watering places" generally fall into social genres reflecting the same classes as the larger society. From Smithville, Rhode Island, to Los Angeles, California, there will be the: hotel/motel bars, business people's lounges, the neighborhood saloon, country western taverns, sports pubs and — just starting to appear on the scene — computer bars. There are also other specialized types having clienteles made up of people of the same race or sexual orientation. Dance lounges vary from those catering to younger rock and rollers, salsa and to ballroom styles for the Arthur Murray types.

There is a pub for just about everyone and you should know by now what I'm going to say next. That is: decide what kind of person you wish to meet and then go to the context where that kind of person will likely be. The woman of your dreams or the man of your fantasies may very well appear in the neighborhood sports bar or that dance lounge just a few blocks away.

### *North to Alaska*

Some find it worthwhile to look to farther-range contexts. Donna Greene, thirty two years old, a kindergarten teacher who is six feet, two inches tall chucked her job in Detroit and opted for Alaska. She had tried many of the near-range places for finding guys, even joining the Skyscraper Club — a social group for tall men and women — but the men were outnumbered by the women six to one! Donna got a teaching position in Anchorage at a military base dependents' school and married an Army Captain within a year of her arrival.

Alaska is a place for tremendous career and social possibilities for young women. With an average age of twenty-five and 132 men for every 100 women, the bargain purchase from Russia beckons the young unmarried damsel in search of her mate. Should the weather and wilderness of the 50$^{th}$ state be too forbidding for some, the cities of San Francisco, Houston and San Diego all have more eligible men than women by a ratio of four to three. For the cities where men would be most likely to meet women, the statistics would have the lady seekers live in Cincinnati, Minneapolis, Newark, Indianapolis, San Antonio or St. Louis where women outnumber men.

### *Looking for Mr. or Mrs. Moneybags*

Someone once said, "the definition of a true miser is a man who would marry Nicole Kidman for her money." Somebody else also has said "it's just as easy to fall in love with someone who's rich as it is for someone who's poor." A third person —

don't ask me who — said, "I've been rich and I've been poor; rich is better." For those inclined to search for a partner with means, the right contexting is crucial.

Joanne Steichen, an author and psychotherapist, advises getting into the social contexts of the wealthy by becoming knowledgeable about the things in which the rich are interested. She suggests learning about art, antiques, endangered animals, horses, dogs, symphony orchestras and charities.

In her book *Marrying Up: An American Dream and Reality*, she urges the reader to attend art galleries, dog and horse shows, antique exhibitions and benefit performances. Also, to volunteer for work in cultural and charitable institutions or get a job where many successful people congregate, such as the office of an investment banker. She, however, cautions against marrying just for money saying "there's no point in spending your life with someone who is going to make you miserable just because you want to marry a status symbol." Sage advice.

Contexting yourself in the company of the kind of person you wish to meet led Penny Antonini, a perky divorcee in her early forties, to take a job as a waitress in the dining room of a prestigious golf club in Naples, Florida. After two years — during which she dated several members — she married one of them. She told me, before they left to reside in Hawaii, that her husband was . . . yes . . . very wealthy, but he was a great guy and a "lot of fun." Penny also added — with a mischievous smile — that she really didn't mind that he was rich.

L.M. Boyd, the nationally-syndicated columnist, relates the experience of Mary X who, after her late husband's funeral, phoned several brokerages to find the best yield for her $10,000 held in low-interest money markets. She soon was receiving invitations to attend stock presentations. She did so, met a variety of guys, and married one of the more affluent. Took her about six months. She then stopped going to the investment introductions. She had achieved her larger goal.

Marrying up — money wise — may not necessarily be what is envisioned. There are those pesky premarital and, more recently, even postmarital agreements — in which one partner may not benefit financially much, or at all, upon a dissolution of the marriage or the death of the spouse.

Marilyn B, a beautiful blonde in her early fifties, married Charles M, a wealthy Chicagoan who was in his late sixties. They connected in the dance lounge of the Ritz Carlton Hotel in Naples, Florida. The groom, in a uniquely romantic gesture, flew the entire band — which had played when they met — to the windy city to perform at the gala wedding reception. Less than two years later, they were divorced. Marilyn appeared on a national TV talk show featuring women who married and divorced wealthy men. She lamented that she got next to nothing from the breakup because of a premarital agreement. Not long after her divorce, Marilyn married her 22-year-old dance instructor.

The ill-fated marriage of the couple featured on the *Who Wants to Marry a Millionaire?* television show of 2000 crumbled almost before the vows were completed. Tying the knot with Mr. Moneybags resulted in no huge financial settlement for the lucky/unlucky finalist of the hundred women who vied for the chance. Again . . . a no gainer because of a premarital deal.

Cliche time: "All that glitters is not gold."

We've talked mostly in this chapter about where women can meet men. How about the reverse? Going back to Marilyn, who met two husbands while dancing, leads to some really good advice for Adams looking for Eves. Men: learn to trip the light fantastic. Generally, most women love to dance and most men would rather have their gums scraped. Proof? How many times have you seen a woman literally (and I do use literally, literally) dragging a man to the dance floor? During the last several years, there were two popular line dances which captured the fancy of night clubbers all over the world: the Electric Slide and the Macarena. When the queues formed, women outnumbered the males ten to one with many instances of an all female lineup. Doesn't matter if the music is rock, disco, Latin, country or ballroom; women love the context of the dance floor. So learn to dance (within-the-nine-dots thinking), or become a dance instructor (beyond the nine dots).

### *IwannaMeetSomeone.com*

Earlier in this chapter, I cited writers in the boy-meets-girl genre who urged that singletons get out of the house to meet prospective mates or friends. Not necessarily so. More and more people are turning to the near-range context of computers in their homes as a dating source. The medium offers a way to learn a lot about potential dates before ever meeting them. Chat rooms or the personals posted usually elicit the person's interests, occupation, salary, smoking preference, religion and age. Having all that information makes it easier to initiate contact with only those who meet the desired requirements. Cyber-dating seems definitely on the rise. Take note of . . .

### *The Swedish Connection*

Mildred Levy, in her late thirties, lives in a villa across the courtyard from me. Divorced several years, she works at home in a computer-based business. Two years ago she met a man via the Internet who met her requirements as a potential mate; he had to be tall, educated, financially secure and orthodox Jewish. He lives in Sweden and has visited her here twice while she's flown to his abode once and is planning another trip this summer. The gossip going around is that wedding bells will soon be ringing and Millie may be moving to Scandinavia or, we may be getting a new Swedish applicant for dual citizenship.

America Online's Bill Schreiner says the company receives about 200 letters a day from people who've had successful romances through the aegis of the Internet. He estimates that AOL is responsible for at least 10,000 marriages and touts the Internet as the way of the future for dating. As mentioned earlier, it's convenient and easy to use. There's also that important safety factor advantage in cyber-dating. Before agreeing to meet, one can verify employment and check other facts. Exchanging e-mail or instant messages a few times can determine the direction of the relationship. If the communication goes south, it's easy to end the dialogue. If necessary, a subscriber can readily change an e-mail address. Thus, one has a great measure of control over the process. As one wag puts it: "You don't have to kiss any frogs along the way."

**The computer may be the biggest of all matchmakers.**

Schreiner's comments are given further credence by noticing that the entertainment industry has quickly picked up on this major trend. The computer got Meg Ryan and Tom Hanks together in the movie *You Have Mail.* A new sitcom debuted in 2002 featuring cyber romances and titled *E-Love.*

### *"SWF Desires to Meet SWM*

For those of you who are not yet into computers (Why aren't you?), there are other effective ways of meeting your significant other. My late brother, Henry, grieved the passing of his first wife, Ida, for six months. They had been married for 35 happy years. Lonesome and very unhappy, he placed an ad in the personals column of the town newspaper in Gastonburg, North Carolina. He stipulated the age bracket (early sixties), desirable common interests (travel, bowling, religion) and had six responses for his one-day posting. He gave his phone number in the ad and conversed with all before mutually agreeing to meet Pauline. With some trepidation felt by both parties, they arranged a date at the local bowling alley. They clicked immediately, were married six months later and enjoyed eight blissful years together. Hank died in 1996 following Pauline's passing a few months earlier.

Another humor break:

(Reprinted with special Permission of King Features Syndicate.)

### *Sex and Contextica*

The where and when of human sexual behavior has always been a fascinating topic. We've discussed some of the dangers of careless choices at the beginning of this chapter. Let's look at another example of incredibly bad contexting. You're going to find this one hard to believe but it really happened.

A professor at Case-Western Reserve University in Cleveland, Ohio, and his wife, liked to make love while she was hanging out the window of their second floor apartment. One night while engaging in their window sill sex, he lost his grip and she plummeted to her death. He was able to prove through friends' testimonies that this was one of the couples' agreed-upon ways of achieving connubial bliss. The investigation of the death resulted in it being judged accidental and the careless husband escaped even a charge of manslaughter. Safety — not just in the sense of health (avoiding diseases) — should be a paramount consideration in choosing the context of lovemaking. While the professor escaped legal retribution for his folly, his standing in the community was irretrievably clouded.

While not nearly as dangerous in the physical sense, Clarence's choice of an exciting context for coitus was also foolhardy. He liked to get it on with his girlfriend in a display tent at the Sports Authority store! No, he wasn't an employee there doing it after closing. He was there as a customer during business hours with the usual number of shoppers walking around. In many towns, they could have been jailed for their mischievous choice if discovered. Clarence is an elementary school teacher and Pattie works as a nurse at the local hospital. Their employers would certainly not have appreciated their free-spirited choice.

Variety really is the spice of life . . . and, of lovemaking. Creatively changing contextica (place and time) increases enjoyment and enhances interest. Of course, common sense must be used; privacy should be maintained and mutual agreement is a must. Getting out of the bedroom once in a while and making it in the car, front porch, shower, a closet or on the kitchen table are exciting alternatives.

Again, the contextica of sex should be consistent with propriety and good manners. What two people do in their sex play — if mutually agreeable and not harmful to anyone — is O.K. as long as the arena is wisely chosen. What may be appropriate in one place may not be in another venue. Our civilized society depends on the ability to understand the subtleties of context. Acceptable behavior is not always an absolute; it varies with the circumstances. On the lighter side:

> A fellow went to his doctor complaining that after eight years of marriage, the love act had degenerated into the same old "boring, humdrum affair." The doctor, reasoning that a change of context would put some spice back into the marital relationship, instructed his patient to go home at lunchtime and surprise his wife by grabbing her and kissing her the moment he was inside the house, tearing off her clothes, and then making mad, passionate love to her right there on the living room carpet!
>
> Several days later, the man returned the to the doctor's office and said he had done exactly as the doctor prescribed. "Well?" asked the doctor. "Well, Doc," the man replied, "it's still the same old boring, humdrum affair . . . *but her bridge club got a tremendous kick out of it!"*

While the living room floor was a good place for a location change, the timing was a bit off. He should have checked his wife's schedule for that day. (By the way, would this story be funnier if we rewrote it using the creativity tool of reversal? How about having the wife come home and seduce the husband before she realized the guy's entire poker group was witnessing the free exhibition?)

A couple of examples of creatively contexting lovemaking drawn from responses to a columnist's request for contest entries describing in one paragraph, "Best Places Where I've Made Love."

The winner and runnerup:

> *For my husband and me, one of our favorites is in the Gulf of Mexico. For us, there is nothing as exciting as making love in water up to our shoulders, surrounded by others unaware of what is going on. Maybe it's the adventure, the aspect of forbidden fruit, or some sort of deep exhibitionist tendency — but making it in a body of water is the zenith of ecstasy . . . the pinnacle of passion. It's definitely one of the most thrilling ways to copulate in public — privately!*

> *On a weekend in Key West, my girlfriend and I did the usual sightseeing: touring the Hemingway house, drinking beer at Sloppy Joe's, and watching the magnificent sunset from the dock at Mallory Square. But the part we'll remember all our lives is our visit to the lighthouse. After ascending the spiral staircase and reaching the observation deck, we were awed by the beautiful panorama. Overcome with emotion, we became passionate and made love knowing we would hear anyone who might be coming up the stairs. What a celebration of life in that unique, lovely setting! Talk about a Rocky Mountain high . . . that was a lighthouse high, figuratively and literally.*

Honorable mentions included: on horseback (not while galloping!), on a tree limb (caution . . . remember the Cleveland professor), in a telephone booth (kinda cramped), and several who claimed membership in the Mile High Club ( having sex during an airplane flight, usually in the restroom . . . again, kinda cramped).

### *Playing in Your Own Back Yard*

The workplace is, of course, where many people find relationships. It's where most of us spend the bulk of our waking hours and it affords the opportunity of getting to know a lot about the men and women there. But, in many cases, the pool of eligible females or males is small or even nonexistent. Debbie Delaney, a lab assistant, found that to be too true. Her interaction at work came only with the four other employees in her department — all happily married. There was some communication with others in the company cafeteria, but she felt uncomfortable about getting into a social relationship with someone from the workplace which might not go well — and seeing an ex-boyfriend each day on the job could be awkward, to say the least. She decided to go beyond the nine-dots area of her job by getting part-time employment as a cocktail waitress at an upscale downtown bar. There she met, dated for almost a year, and married Art Seward, a sales rep for Hewlett-Packard.

**There's a very thin line between honest courting and sexual harassment.**

While the workplace will always be a context where social unions are begun, there are two red flag words of caution which didn't exist with today's magnitude just a generation ago . . . sexual harassment. There have been many successful and costly law suits resulting from a co-worker's unwelcome amorous advances. Companies have responded by developing policies regarding fraternization among employees. Superordinate-subordinate liaisons are especially susceptible to possible misinterpretation. There is now a very thin and vague line between honest-to-goodness, well-intentioned courting and sexual harassment. Remember Supreme Court Justice Clarence Thomas's nomination problems when his law clerk accused him of sexual harassment? Remember the movie in which Demi Moore's boss character was sued by her underling, played by a hapless Michael Douglas?

And who can forget the case in 1999 of the 6-year-old boy who kissed a classmate on the cheek only to be charged with sexual harassment? The "Tailhook" scandal of that same year has left all the armed forces with an increased sensitivity and concern about male-female relations in their ranks.

Thus, in the age-old battle of the genders, what was once accepted as part of life's games has now become a matter of official action. It is definitely a time of "suitors beware!" Certainly it is smart to heed the admonition *"look before you leap!"*

### *Age and Sex*

Sexperts generally agree that the male of the human species peaks, physiologically, in the late teens while the female does so in her early thirties. Why Mother Nature set it up that way is a puzzlement, but I'm sure she had her reasons. It's also fairly well established that the optimum fertility age for men is 26 and for women, 24. That makes more sense. With age, sex behavior invariably changes but it stays as a vital part of our lives from the early teens through very old age. Unlike all the other animals of our species, we not only can copulate from the adolescent through the geriatric years but we can also get it on during any of the twelve months of the year, eschewing any temporal "mating season." Considering the puberty years as the beginning of our sex lives (discounting some Freudian theories) and assuming a human life span approaching eighty years, we can generalize that the descendants of Adam and Eve can enjoy lovemaking for — give or take — *sixty-five years*!

The last decade of the nineties will be known for many events and one of them will surely be the pharmaceutical debut of sex-life-enhancing pills. Viagra was the first which enabled men to prolong — some kind of pun *is* intended here — their erectile function capability. At this writing, work is apace to develop the same kind of aid for women. Let's hope that comes about soon for it still — I promise this will absolutely be the only cliche on this page — "takes two to Tango."

Relating our sexual behavior to the various time contexts of our lives elicits some disturbing tidings when we look at the initial years. Teenagers engaging in full and frequent, unprotected intercourse are one of the world's worst problems. The statistics concerning the numbers of babies born from unwed, irresponsible, uncaring teenage couples are awesome. More than a million teens become pregnant each year in the United States and about one in three of those conceptions is aborted, according to the Medical Institute for Sexual Health. Of the children born, 72 percent have no married parents, which usually means the fathers have abdicated their

**72 percent of teenagers' babies have unwed parents.**

responsibilities. The many social problems so engendered are exacerbated by an accompanying critical health crisis among young people. A United Nations AIDS expert commenting on the crisis in Africa says that in Botswana, *two-thirds of children will be dead of the disease before they have reached their sixteenth birthday*!

That last statement is so incredible, it bears repeating . . . so I'll repeat it: *two of every three children will never reach their sixteenth birthday having perished in the previous years!* While Botswana is the extreme example, most other sub-Saharan nations are also in serious trouble and are frantically attempting to institute programs which warn young people of the dangers of unprotected and promiscuous sexual encounters.

Although Africa is the center of the crisis, AIDS is now spreading very rapidly in Europe, Asia, the Caribbean and the United States. Our country now has the highest rate of infection (1.7 percent of Americans carry the AIDS virus) of industrialized nations. We do live in a global society in which planes and ships are transporting people every hour of every day from all areas to all other areas. When it comes to communicable diseases . . . no country is an island.

In the United States, adolescents (10-19) are among the two age groups which are most at risk for acquiring sexually transmitted diseases. The other is young adults (20-24). In the Jacksonville, Florida area, there are over 1300 pregnancies among teens each year. According to the *1999 Statistical Abstract of the United States,* one of every five births among whites, blacks, American Indian and Hispanics, collectively, is from a teenage mother. Rhea County, Tennessee, executive Billy Ray Patton — who served on the school board for 13 years — lamented that the teenage pregnancy rate approached 40 percent in the schools before they undertook action to reduce that figure by encouraging abstinence. Thirteen, fourteen and fifteen-year-old students were — and are — getting pregnant . . . mere *children* having children.

Thus, the teen decade is the time context fraught with many problems and challenges. We want our sons and daughters to develop and enjoy healthy relationships with the opposite gender. But we certainly don't want to see them scar their early lives with abortions, unwanted and unprepared-for children, or getting one of the more than 25 sexually transmitted diseases that are surely out there. The twenties and thirties are the most important decades for sexual activity. In those years, procreative activity is at its zenith as we strive to reproduce ourselves and carry the human race onward to . . . wherever. Mother Nature continues to puzzle us, however, when we look at yet another seeming discrepancy between the sexes. The male's ability to achieve orgasm is fairly constant throughout most of his sex life while the female's varies with different ages. A 1994 University of Chicago study found that women in their early twenties are the *least* likely of all age groups to attain orgasm during intercourse! It's a fortunate fact for the human race that conception is not dependent on orgasm.

More recent research would suggest that is also the case with females in their teens. In a poll of hundreds of students in the Rhea County schools in 1998, researcher Cathi Woods found that 79% of boys responded to the question: "Why are you having sex?" by selecting "Because it feels good." *Not a single female chose that answer*! Since orgasm has to be one of

**In the thirties, the libidinal gender gap begins to lessen.**

the most "feel good" sensations that we can have, it's probably safe to say those teen girls are not yet experiencing it. One explanation, by Judith Seifer, past president of the American Association of Sex Educators, Counselors and Therapists, on why men and women in their twenties are often sexually incompatible is that, in those years, the male wants novelty without commitment while the female craves devotion and stability. Men pursue as many partners as possible and women attempt to select the strongest and healthiest mate of those who can protect their offspring.

In the thirties, this libidinal gender gap begins to lessen as women begin to feel the need for more physical pleasure from genital sex. According to Dr. Theresa Crenshaw, author of *The Alchemy of Love and Lust,* hormonal changes occur as testosterone levels increase resulting in greater assertiveness and interest in orgasm. The thirties, it appears, may be considered as the sexually liberating decade for women.

During their forties, men and women have usually arrived at a level of rapprochement based on experience and having attained a greater measure of emotional maturity. Gone, or at least greatly diminished, is the battling between the sexes. The female's likelihood of orgasms is the highest in this decade. This, attributable largely to the groundbreaking gains made by women in the last few decades, not only in education and employment, but in the quantum-leap changes in our cultural mores. Unlike their Victorian counterparts, it became O.K. for females to shed their angst and actually enjoy sex. What an epiphany!

The fifties are characterized by Crenshaw as "relaxed and romantic." There is extra time, and usually more privacy, for couples to enjoy lovemaking more fully. Although the frequency of male erections drops slightly, this is well compensated for by longer tumescence time. Women, generally, experience a decrease in lubrication in the genital area which prescribes that more foreplay is necessary. Use of a vibrator may be helpful. This also coincides happily with the male's now longer erection durations.

For the sixties and succeeding decades, sex continues to be an enjoyable and vital part of our lives. While the frequency will decrease, the pleasure may be consequently enhanced. Continuing sexual activity into the later decades may be a major factor in leading a longer life. Doctors advise men to lead active sex lives as a preventive for prostate cancer. One urologist puts it rather whimsically: "Keep flowing in those pipes or they'll rust out." Makes sense.

**The longer you love, the longer you'll live.**

Curiously, the exercise value of the sex act is rarely mentioned or appreciated. Obviously, it activates muscles, moves joints in the skeletal structure, gets the heart pumping, gives the lungs a workout and affords a lot of fun in the process. Besides providing pleasurable calisthenics, there's also an accompanying mental health aspect. Orgasm is the ecstatic release of not only a physical tension but an emotional one as well. It is the ultimate catharsis. I suspect few doctors and health professionals would disagree . . . the longer you love, the longer you'll live.

Our sexual behaviors, in summary, are strongly influenced by our time contexts (ages). Knowing more about how they relate can give us valuable insight as to how to enjoy a physically satisfying, health-giving, and emotionally fulfilling sex role at just about any age.

### *Timing and Sex*

Synchronicity. What a beautiful word! It connotes the coming together of differing elements at just the right time to blend into a desirable result. When a symphony orchestra is in synch, it is a joy to listen. When it is not, the result is dissonance, disharmony — an assault to our ears.

The same holds true in our sex lives. Just as there were wrong places for lovemaking discussed earlier in this chapter (the window sill, the tent), there are wrong times for sex. The goal for couples should be to initiate sex when it is desired by <u>both</u> partners. This involves knowing and appreciating the different moods and idiosyncrasies of the other person.

> It was the second marriage for Sonya and Jim Barnes, both in their early sixties. A few months after their honeymoon, Jim felt some unease with their sex life. Sonya liked to stay up late watching the 11o'clock news and then flipping channels between Jay Leno and David Letterman until she would finally nod off at around 1a.m. — hours after her husband had entered dreamland. Jim had always been an "early to bed, early to rise" sleeper. The frequency of sexual intercourse had decreased to about twice a month from their courting weeks' rate of two and even three times a week. Jim became irritable about the situation and Sonya, in turn, became irritable about Jim's irritability. What to do?

Applying our **FOUR STEP PLAN** to this situation could have this scenario. In a ***Self Analysis*** the couple would sit down and talk frankly about the problem, jointly agreeing that there is something lacking in the union. Admissions by both that their sex life is not ***as good as it gets*** would lead to an assessment of the seriousness of the problem. Has it gotten to the place where the ***"pain"*** of the sex area of the relationship potentially threatens the ***"pleasure"*** of the marriage as a whole? Is the unhappiness of one partner reaching a tipping point? If so, it's really a problem for both.

Once there is agreement that a problem exists, then the couple should decide on ***setting a goal.*** In this case, that might be "increasing the frequency of sex to at least once per week" which for Sonya and Jim seemed ***realistic, achievable*** and easily ***measurable.*** But you may remember — or you may not — from the chapter on goal-setting, that the goal should not be too narrow (Jody Cantor's "seek a higher-paying job"). For the Barnes, the broader goal could be "improving the sex aspect of our marriage so that we will make love at least once a week." This is more encompassing and allows for other than just a quantitative improvement although that would be the measure for attainment. It can reasonably be assumed that improving the quality of their lovemaking will also happily result in an increase in the frequency of intercourse. The goal is ***realistic***, ***achievable*** and ***measurable.*** It then becomes a contract for the partners, with each committed to its attainment. Finally, the couple needs to record it and set a time frame. Recording may be simply putting a note of reminder on the refrigerator. An appropriate time line could be six months.

Then comes the ***Self Start*** in which the couple explores all the possible ways to achieve the goal. This involves selecting, from our arsenal of creative thinking strategies, the method (or methods) that seems most appropriate. We have: IDEATIONAL FLUENCY (BRAINSTORMING), CHECKLISTING, FORCED RELATIONSHIPS, MORPHOLOGICAL ANALYSIS and FREE ASSOCIATION.

Let's use IDEATIONAL FLUENCY and a CHECKLIST as a way Sonya and Jim could come up with their plan. Remember, in brainstorming there is no such thing as a ridiculous or impossible suggestion. Freewheeling and hitchhiking on someone else's thoughts are encouraged. We're going for quantity first and then we'll work our way to quality and what is actually doable. The more far out or ludicrous the entries, the better.

This should be a fun undertaking with a lot of good-natured humor involved as we look at how the couple, in a joint effort, could apply some creative thinking to their vexing problem. I've left plenty of space between each item for you to make your own additions to the listings. (What? You don't want to write in a book. O.K., use a separate sheet of paper. I like to use a publication as a workbook. I scribble in the margins, highlight sentences or paragraphs, tear out pages, and dog-ear certain sections with the philosophy that the book is for me . . . I am not for the book.) Feel free to hitchhike on their ideas. Try to make two or three additions to each category.

**Goal for Sonya and Jim Barnes**

*"Improve the sex part of our marriage so that we will make love at least once a week."*

**Adapt . . .**

- our time schedule for sex by setting a specific hour and day for lovemaking.

- don't set a time, agree to make overtures at any time — even in the middle of the night.
- make our bedroom more "sex friendly" . . . put mirrors on the ceiling/walls.
- change bulbs for mood lighting, light candles, put in tv/vcr for "romantic" movies.

**Combine . . .**

- lovemaking with our other activities: have sex during showering, swimming, walks, exercising, bicycling, gardening, meal preparation, traveling.
- saving fund for a vacation or new car with sex frequency by agreeing to put $10, $20, or $50 into a cookie jar for each love session.

**Eliminate . . .**

- repressions by consenting that anything we do as a couple which is mutually agreeable, enjoyable and not harmful is O.K.
- distractions such as the phone ringing . . . disconnect it.

**Magnify . . .**

- magnify the time spent on foreplay, make it eightplay (double the time).

**Minify . . .**

- minify activities which may make us too tired for sex.

**Modify . . .**

- modify our wardrobes to include sex-enhancing night wear, costumes.

**Put to Other Uses . . .**

- think of all lovemaking sessions as really great and beneficial exercise.
- make a vow that all our arguments should end with lovemaking.

**Reverse . . .**

- intercourse positions, time of making love from late night to early morning.

- alternate initiating sex by each partner. [hitchhike: alternate places]

**Substitute . . .**

- watching a weekly television program (*60 Minutes)* for sex.
- [hitchhike: agree to make love <u>during</u> the program]
- make love in place of walking the treadmill . . .
- [hitchhike: have sex <u>on</u> the treadmill]
- quit membership at the exercise club; substitute it with sexual exercise.

After listing as many possibilities as they could, it's time to let the right halves of their brains rest while they switch over to the practical left hemispheres of that wonderful organ. Reality, legality, feasibility, and safety are all considered as they decide which of the time and place contexts are right for them. It should go without saying, but I'll say it anyway: both parties must be in complete agreement upon the final choices. It really does [fill in the spaces] take ____ to _______.

And now, of course, comes the fun part — the implementation of their plan over the next six months. We'll not attempt here any description of the couples' activities in pursuit of their goal. The purpose of this book is — not to appeal to any prurient interests — but to encourage creative strategies for solving life's problems. Sorry to disappoint, but I wouldn't attempt to compete in any way with the many fine writers in that genre.

Chances are that Sonya and Jim will have achieved their goal well before the six-month period. Perhaps after a few weeks they would have been agreeing that the situation had greatly improved and they could then evaluate their undertaking as a ***success*** with that accompanying feeling of —

***— how sweet it is!***

## Chapter Eight

## TIME REALLY IS OF THE ESSENCE

**"So much to do, and so little time."**
**— Cecil Rhodes**

Each of us has our own unique and intimate relationship with our total environment {place) and the two interact in a mysterious dimension (time). Both — our place and our time — have been termed, our contextica. The human condition can be simply defined as the interplay of those three factors: the individual, environment and time.

But what is this thing called time? World-renowned physicist Stephan Hawking, in his *A Brief History of Time,* refers to time as "whatever that is." Another physicist, Albert Einstein, seemed to understand it but few people understand him. He did establish that it is somehow bound up with space and matter, but a full grasp of that is probably held just by fellow scientists and some others like Marilyn Vos Savant. The *Oxford Dictionary* defines it as "one of the dimensions of the physical world in which we live." Not much help in comprehending that intangible but very real phenomenon. Lawyers insist that it is "the essence" of any contract.

At the turn of the 5th century A.D., St. Augustine wrote:

> *For what is time? Who can readily and briefly explain this? Who can even in thought comprehend it,*

*so as to utter a word about it? But what in discourse do we mention more familiarly and knowingly than time? And, we understand, when we speak of it; when we understand also, when we hear it spoken of by another. What then is time? If no one asks me, I know; if I wish to explain it to one that asketh, I know not.*

And so, while we all know what time it *is*, none of us seems to really know what time itself is; nonetheless, we have done a remarkable job of measuring it. We've parsed it into nanoseconds, seconds, minutes, hours, days, weeks, months, years, decades, centuries, millennia, and aeons. Interestingly, three of those are based on natural phenomena while all the others have been artificially arrived at. The day is, of course, a measurement based on one revolution of the earth on its axis while the month relates to the moon's movement around our planet, and the year is the time it takes to fly our earth ship around the sun.

**None of us really knows what time itself is.**

The measurement of time began about four thousand years ago with the first clock in the form of a sundial. Since then, it has been said, more machines to measure time have been built than all other machines combined. I believe that. Think about it. You may have two or three television sets, one or two automobiles, or four or five telephones, but when it comes time to reset timepieces to accommodate daylightsavings time changes, you probably have more than a dozen — alarms, wristwatches, clock-radios, microwave, stove, tv, vcr, car, etc.

The sundial proved not very efficient given the fickleness of sunshine and cloud cover and the variations of days/nights in different regions. Consequently, creative people like you (yes, *you*) came up with better methods by using: sand in hourglasses, liquid in water devices, pent-up energy in windup chronometers, and tiny batteries in wristwatches. . . which reminds me of this little story.

> A very frugal and time-conscious fellow, having a drink with his friend, noticed that his wristwatch had stopped. Observing that his companion's watch was running, he said: "The battery in my Bulova must be dead. Do you have a very, very teeny set of jumper cables?"

But enough about the history or measurement of time. That's really not our province here. For those who hunger for more on that topic, I commend you to Jo Ellen Barnett's excellent book, *Time's Pendulum.* (Plenum Publishing Corp.)

Our concern here is with appreciating the *enormous* importance of the time aspect of our contextica and in creatively choosing right times and avoiding wrong times. While we cannot control time — "time management" is a misnomer — we *can* master ourselves in relation to it.

We can't create or alter the mysterious dimension. It — "whatever it is" — comes to us all equally while we're alive. Whether we are rich or poor, male or female, Americans or Indonesians, black, brown, red, or white; Muslim, Jewish, or Christian; living in Paris or Des Moines — we *all* get the *same* twenty-four hours per day (with the possible exceptions of the first and last days of our lives). No more, no less.

When the question is asked: "What is the most important thing in life?" The response is usually "good health," "peace of mind," "doing good works," "family."

But I submit to you that all of those are wrong. *The most important thing you and I have is time.* Without it, none of the rest mentioned can exist. Thus, time becomes synonymous with life. We should all, then, heed the wise counsel of Saroyan when he writes: "In the time of your life, live." There is, *really*, only one age — "alive."

Our life term varies from zero or a few minutes (childbirth deaths) to a reported 130 years, with the average life span somewhere in the late seventies here in the good old U. S. of A. The spatial aspect of our contextica is something we can exercise control over for most of our lives; the temporal factor is definitely finite. We are — in those grim words — "born to die" and while we can change *where* we live at just about any age, we have no say at all about *how long* we may live. Tomorrow is never guaranteed. All that any of us can be sure of is that we have the present fleeting moment. And fleeting it is. If I were to ask you what time it is and you glance at your chronometer and tell me most accurately that it is ten minutes and thirty seconds past twelve o'clock, as soon as you've said it, it's history . . . no longer accurate.

Yes, time (existence) is our most precious possession. Like any possession, it can be well spent or misused, handled wisely or foolishly. Worst of all, it can be wasted. And in today's wondrous world of fantastic technological achievements, the temptation to waste this irreplaceable gift is greater than ever. We daily confront so many options that it is increasingly difficult to make positive selections of our contextica. It's quite an irony that although we live in an age of incredible achievements, that very condition may hinder the creative potential inherent in all of us.

**The most important thing you and I have is . . . time.**

In an earlier chapter we've reviewed what forms those hindrances may take: couch/recliner potatoes, TV/remote potatoes, sports fan potatoes, golf cart potatoes, movie/video rental potatoes, computer mouse potatoes, etc. There *is* a sure solution to the dilemma:

## Prioritizing Your Time

At a conference on leadership conducted in Atlantic City a few years ago, Dr. Louis Krinsky, the speaker — whose topic was that misnomer *Time Management* — gave this demonstration.

> He placed a large, wide-mouth jar on the table in front of him. He produced a dozen or so fist-sized rocks and placed them one at a time into the glass receptacle. When the jar was filled to the top and no more rocks would fit inside, he asked: "Is this jar full?"
>
> The entire group yelled, "Yes."
>
> The speaker replied, "Really?" He reached under the table and brought out a bucket of gravel. He poured some gravel in and shook the jar so the pellets could work themselves between the spaces of the big rocks. He asked again, "Is the jar full?"
>
> By this time some of the audience were on to him and there was a mixed response of yeas and nays. He reached under the table again and produced a bucket of fine sand and proceeded to pour it into the spaces between the rocks and the gravel. Again he queried, "Now, is this jar finally full?" More mixed responses. He then grabbed a pitcher of water and poured into the jar until it was filled to the brim.

> He then challenged the group, "What is the point of this demonstration?" One participant offered that, "No matter how full your schedule, if you really try you can fit more in." "Very good," he replied, "but the bigger point here is that if you don't put the big rocks in first, you'll never get them in at all. What are the 'big rocks' in your life — time with your loved ones, your education, your dreams, your job, your faith?" Prioritize your dreams and aspirations keeping in mind if they are rocks, gravel, sand or water.

I've always remembered Dr. Krinsky's entertaining and informative session and have used the example many times in workshops on creative thinking. Tuck it into your remembery. Try to think of it every morning as you throw off the covers and greet your precious new day. Think: rocks, gravel, sand and water.

Let's now look at a model of how one couple could apply creative (and logical — remember, they're complementary) thinking to their lives. I've given you some examples of the applications of: FORCED RELATIONSHIPS, MORPHOLOGICAL ANALYSIS (MATRIXING), CHECKLISTING and FREE ASSOCIATION (BRAINSTORMING, DREAMING). In this instance the primary technique will be IDEATIONAL FLUENCY although, as you will discern, there is a great deal of overlapping.

Although this is a hypothetical example, it does relate to an increasingly evident problem in American society.

## Randy and Louise

For the first time since the Census Bureau has kept the record, families in which both parents work have become the majority based on data from 1998. That majority held even among the most traditional families: married couples with children. In that year, almost 60 percent of women with babies younger than a year old were working, more than twice the percentage of a generation ago.

Louise and Randy had been married eight years. She worked as a nurse and Randy was a marketing director for a carpet manufacturing company. Both jobs were located in downtown Atlanta, Georgia. They have two children: Beth, age six, and Larry, age three. Louise earned $45,000 per year while her husband pulled down $82,000. The family resided in a new four-bedroom, three-bath home in an upper middle class eastern suburb. They each drove late model cars: she a Lexus and he a Ford SUV. Their combined salaries of almost $130,000 were stretched because of a heavy mortgage, car payments, medical bills, taxes, insurance and final payments on a student loan made for Louise's nurse education.

They enjoyed their new home and the many comforts of life they had been able to accumulate but both felt an unease with their lifestyle. A continuing concern was that their family life was suffering — that they were not spending enough time with Beth and Larry. They felt guilty about having the three-year-old in a daycare setting. The golden years of early childhood, they lamented, were slipping away quickly and they were shortchanging the kids.

Randy and Louise had several of these ***Self Analysis*** discussions before they finally agreed that a tipping point had been reached. Randy was asked to take on additional responsibilities, which would mean a promotion and raise in pay but would entail more evenings away from home. Because of a critical lack of nurses, Beth was also constantly being requested to put in more hours. They decided to ***Set a Goal*** of "spending more time with our children." More specifically, they would strive to double the time during the next year in which the children were with at least one parent.

At no time was a child to be without at least one of the parents except for attendance at school. They determined that a secure and happy family life was their highest priority. That rock was going into the jar first.

Their goal was achievable, measurable and had a time frame of one year. They recorded it as a banner on their computer personal page so as to be regularly reminded. Remember, we want our goals to be realistic, measurable, definite — time wise — and recorded.

The couple began their ***Self Start*** by sitting down and thinking about all the things they could do to achieve their goal by using the technique of FREE ASSOCIATION — brainstorming. To review that method, we all remember — don't we? — that it involves solving a problem by listing all the possible ideas *(freewheeling)* that we can conjure without any regard as to their practicality. We're looking for *quantity* at this stage, not quality. Even the most ridiculous comments are listed as they may lead to a more viable possibility. This *hitchhiking* is strongly encouraged as it provides even more options.

Most of us probably use personal brainstorming when confronted with a problem. Alone, we free associate when we think: "What if I do this?" Louise and Randy will have the advantage of two minds acting together with the one encouraging the other. They could also choose to do a larger group session by inviting friends — other couples with similar interests — to participate. The more individuals involved, the more ideas will be *recorded* and the chances of arriving at the best solutions are then greatly enhanced. (It is very important that ideas be written or otherwise recorded.)

A final point here is that once a session is seemingly finished, it is not. The participant(s) should continue to add to the list either immediately or at another session. Several sessions are ideal. Remember our illustration of the star and cubes? The more you look, the more you'll see. The more sessions devoted to the problem, the better. It's amazing how many additional ideas will come up once the process has started — sometimes in the middle of the night. The endeavor should not be rushed. After all, the astute car-shopper doesn't buy the first vehicle looked at.

Let's see what Louise and Randy's brainstorming sessions might have produced. Be a part of it. Feel free to add any ideas you may get as you hitchhike on the items listed. There's plenty of space allowed for you to do this. Write in a book! Sure. Remember the book is for you, you are not for the book.

Here we go. Forget about spelling or punctuation. Just get it down.

Randy and Louise's Brainstorming Sessions
Goal: Spend more time with our children.

one quits job

one works part-time

both work part-time

either one takes a sabbatical leave

both take leaves of absence

alternate years of work

nurse quits hospital and does private duty

develop a home business for one or both
lower living standards so that both do not have to work

both keep jobs but hire housekeeper and landscaper to take care of all domestic chores... so as to allow more time for parent-children togetherness

so as to make up for loss of income by one...
play the lottery more, rob a bank, get parents to give some of the inheritance now, move to a smaller house, move to a bigger house and start a home business as an assisted care facility, sell one car, sell both cars... use public transportation, move to Montana

Randy works days...Louise can do the night shift at the hospital or work three 12-hour shifts for the same pay and benefits

invite grandparent(s)to move in
align work schedules to coincide with school vacations

home-school the children     join a commune
buy and live on a farm

move to a small town and open a bread and breakfast inn

There you have it. Those possibilities — plus the ones you added (You did, didn't you?) — should provide plenty of food for thought as Louise and Randy move towards a solution to their problem. Now it is time for them to select and then implement the one or ones that seem most appropriate for them. What path will they choose? No two people can ever see a rainbow the same way. Each of us is in our own center of that circular spectrum of color. So Louise and Randy will have to agree on what will be best for their family, examining the pros and cons of each option. Will they stay in their present location and jobs doing some things to increase time with the kids, or make a big leap like moving to that town with the bed and breakfast? Whatever they decide, at the very least, they will have applied creative thinking to better the quality of the children's and their lives. ***Success*** will surely follow.

### This 'n That...Right Times, Wrong Times

We'll conclude this chapter with a listing of some generally accepted right times and wrong times to do things. They've been collected over the years from reading, research, personal experience and the application of good common sense. Of course, many of them are subject to individual preferences. As an example: when I list the best and worst times for men to go to the barber shop or women to the hairdresser, my criterion is... the least time spent waiting. Many people don't really mind — even look forward to — sitting and reading magazines they wouldn't have at home. Remember the long-distance commuters to workplaces who actually enjoy their hours of driving because they like the solitude, listening to the radio or playing CDs? Others — of the listings — are pretty much self-proving or commonsensical. If I were to have serious surgery and the doctor did eight of those operations a day, I don't think I'd like to be number eight on the schedule. She might be a little tired after the other seven. I'd really rather have her operate on me first thing in the morn after she's had breakfast and is fresh and ready to go. Make sense?

Another caveat: most of the listings provide some important and helpful guidance in helping you to choose right — and avoid wrong — times. Others may not make any sense at all. I included them only because they're interesting or funny. Also, these listings are suggestive. It's up to you to make up your own choices.

**On Matters of Health and Safety**

- Wrong time to start a diet to lose weight is spring. That's when more food is needed to sustain our bodies. Our physiques don't react well to cutbacks in that season.

- Best time to diet [to lose weight] is after 3:00 P.M. One of the proven ways of losing weight quickly and significantly is to eat *nothing* after that hour. Worst time is to eat just before retiring.

- Most dangerous time for people with heart conditions, far and away, is Monday morning. Riskiest time for myocardial infarction is within two or three hours of awakening. Heart attacks occur at a 33 percent higher rate than on the other six days. Blood clots, also, are much more likely to happen in mornings.

- Least painful time to have dental work done is early morning when our tolerance for discomfort is highest. Avoid late afternoon or evening appointments.

- Wrong time to jog or do outdoor exercise in congested areas is during morning and evening rush hours when ozone and carbon monoxide levels are highest. Right times, then, would be in early morning and late evening hours away from heavily traveled streets or roads.

- Safest time to drive is Sunday morning — nine hours after the most dangerous period which is late Saturday and early Sunday morning. Most fatal accidents happen between 11:00 P.M. Saturday and 4:00 A.M. on Sunday. Worst time to ride your motorcycle is between 6:00 and 9:00 on Saturday evenings when most motorcycle deaths occur. Same time for most deaths of pedestrians.

- Mondays, after the spring shift to daylight-saving time, usually record a jump in automobile accidents — perhaps because of the loss of an hour's shut-eye. Accidents go down on the driving day after the shift back to standard time when we get an extra hour of snoozing.

- Drive the less congested roads.

- Nearsighted and elderly tennis players should avoid competing at night. As much as 70 percent of peripheral vision is lost and it's much harder to follow the ball.

- Never order fish in a restaurant on Mondays. According to a respected New York chef, it may be three days old. Best freshest day is Tuesday.

- Try never to go to a hospital in July. That's when the new interns start and have to work horrendous schedules. They're overworked and subject to fatigue and mistakes.

- Right time to buy shoes is in the evening when your feet are somewhat swollen. You're more likely to get a better fit.

- On a grim note...December is the month you're most likely to be strangled, poisoned or shot — according to crime statistics from the Federal Bureau for Investigation.

## Regarding Relationships

- Best times for singles to meet other singles is Friday evening and Saturday morning at video-rental and supermarket stores.

- Right time to initiate sex with pregnant women is during the second trimester when interest is the highest. Wrong times are during the first and last trimesters when interest is very low.

- Best time for men to conceive is winter when their sperm count is highest.

- Most divorces are filed after the last youngster leaves home.

- Most illicit affairs (is that a contradiction in terms?) are carried on between noon and 3:00 P.M. Spouses may get suspicious if they observe the other is selecting special underwear in the morning.

- The fewest divorces and the fewest marriages occur in January.

## Pertaining to Work

- Best times to interview for a job are: first thing in the morning or last hour of the day. The psychological advantages of primacy or recency come into play. We tend to remember the first of anything: first car, first love. . .last movie, last meal, etc. Worst time is just before lunch.

- Most productive workday is Tuesday, least is Friday. Least efficient work hours are before lunch and quitting time.

- Best time to fire someone is last hour of the work week. Worst is Monday morning.

- In making a presentation, first fifteen minutes are most important. Most make up their minds by then.

- Worst month to submit manuscripts to editors is August.

- Wrong time to invade Russia (as Napoleon and Hitler found out) is winter.

- Right time to get a teaching position is in early August. Principals are back from summer vacations and must fill vacancies by opening of school.

## It's Your Money

- Best month to buy a house is December and the best time to sell a house is in May, June and July.

- Clever way to get the most favorable negotiated price at flea markets is to wait until the last hour of the last day. Vendors want to pack the least they can back to their vans.

- Never buy stocks before a long weekend.

- Buy a car on the last day of the month. Salespersons may be feverishly trying to make their quota and are more likely to sharpen the pencil. Get a new car at the end of the summer or in early fall just before the next year's new models come out.

- Right time to phone the Internal Revenue Service or Social Security Administration is late in the week. Wrong time is Monday morning. Generally true in phoning most businesses and organizations.

- Try to make purchases of: home appliances in January, furniture in June, carpeting in May, and sheets and linens in January.

- A historical — not hysterical — look at the stock market shows that September and October are usually low points in stock prices (Right time to buy?) and November, December and January are traditionally high price level months (Profit taking opportunity?). But, please, read that with a lot of caution. The stock market's behavior in the last decade of the preceding century and the first year of this one have made many analysts run for cover.

## Peace of Mind

- Try to avoid flying on Thursdays. That's the busiest day of the week for airports. Make airline reservations in early mornings or weekends. Early morning flights are least likely to be canceled.

- Go to hairdressers or barbers on Thursdays for quickest service. Avoid Fridays and Saturdays to elude long waits.

- To avert shopping crowds, go in the mornings. That's when the stores are least congested. Even the week before Christmas, they're navigable before noon. Home Depot managers tell me the least crowded hours are early morning and late evening and the slowest days are Thursdays.

- Right time to go fishin' is very early or late in the day. Wrong time to angle is in the afternoon.

- For golfers, best day to get a tee time is Tuesday. Worst: weekends.

- Hate waiting in long lines at the post office? According to some post office managers, avoid Mondays and Fridays. Thursdays are the slowest.

As I mentioned before, the above is drawn from various research sources, personal experience and just common sense. You may not agree with some of the statements or they may even have changed by now. The important point of all the above is that there *are* right times and wrong times for everyone. Giving more attention as to how you use *your most valuable resource* should merit your highest priority. Once the day is gone, it's gone forever . . . it really is.

Time to move on. Let's close this chapter with a chuckle about a really incredible wrong time and place.

***Before we begin***
***. . . have you heard the one about the priest, rabbi and minister?***

## Chapter Nine

# THE CONTEXTICA OF MONEY

**"Time Is Money."**
**— Ben Franklin**

### *While You Are Sleeping*

Shh, shh, shh, shh...listen. Can you hear a clock ticking? Or look at the second hand on your wristwatch. For every second, minute, hour of the day — time *is* affecting your wealth. It's either *increasing* or *decreasing* your financial position. If you own a house or other real estate, the value is appreciating (or, heaven forbid — depreciating) as you read these lines. Stock prices are going up or down. Your certificates of deposit and savings accounts are accruing interest on your behalf, but your unpaid credit card balances are amassing debts. Even though Franklin was notorious for overdrawing his bank account, his observation is right on. Money and time are partners who work together for or against you.

Each of us has a certain amount of wealth which may be in the form of actual cash; checking or savings accounts; equity in a home, car, boat or other property; ownership of stocks, bonds, IRA's; possession of precious currency, works of art, or other collectibles. This wealth may have been accumulated by: working for it, marrying it, inheriting it, shrewdly investing it, frugal living, hitting the lottery, or any combination of those. Other possibilities are: gambling (yeah, right...I have never ever known a gambler who could make a living, except for being the bookie), defrauding others or armed, or even unarmed, robbery in which case I hope they got this book from the prison library. No matter the size of the estate — from having just enough to keep the wolf from the door or millions stashed away in Swiss bank accounts — it will increase or decrease in its contextica as (1) a function of time and (2) where it is placed. Let's look at two hypothetical but truly representative examples of good and bad money contextica.

### *Dudley DoWrong*

Typical of a majority of credit card holders, Dudley regularly carries a balance on his *Visa*. He pays the minimum amount required on a usual debt of approximately $3,000. (*Debt Counselors of America* reports average credit-card debt in 2000 was $2814.) His card company is delighted to charge interest at the rate of 14% per annum which usually comes out to about $35.00 per month. His after-tax pay from his job is barely $70.00 a day. Dudley works a half day every month for *Visa*'s benefit. Over a year's time his interest on unpaid balances amounts to 420 bucks which is equivalent to six days of his hard-earned wages. He labors over a week of his work year for the money lenders!

### *Rachel Wise*

Rachel, on the other hand, is the credit card companies' lesser preferred customer. She always pays her charges in full every month, never letting one penny of interest accrue. Instead of starting the year with a debt of three grand like Dudley, she invests a like amount — and adds $35 monthly — into a mutual stock fund which increased 14% over the year. At the end of one year, Rachel's $3000 with added monthly deposits of $35 plus compounded interest had grown to the very tidy sum of $3863. At the same time poor Dudley is still $3000 in hock.

Wrong money contextica for Dudley. Wise (pun *is* intended) use of contextica by Rachel.

### *Good Debt, Bad Debt*

Of course we live in a credit economy and the prudent use of debt allows us to have and enjoy things we might never be able to get if we had to first pay in full for them. Good debt can also create wealth when it is used to finance a business venture or to purchase property. Even the very wealthy make use of debt. You think Donald Trump paid for his new properties with his own money? Thus the passage of time enhances or diminishes wealth. You work hard for your money, you should then let your money work for you by using the right contextica for it. Rachel knows that, Dudley doesn't.

How many of us could own a home were it not for the invention of the mortgage? We can have our $300,000 castle for only $30,000 of our own money. We gladly pay the six or eight percent interest because we can possess something immediately that would otherwise take decades to attain. Never mind that each second, minute, hour, day and month is costing us financially. That is greatly overridden by the real benefits of home ownership, not the least of which is *appreciation* where time begins to work in our favor. More about that later in this chapter.

As to *where* to place your money so that time can do its magical work for you? There have never been more options available... a veritable wealth of choices. We have: checking and savings accounts; certificates of deposit; money market funds; the stock and bond markets; IRA's; precious metals; works of art; antiques; coins; memorabilia; real estate; etc. Or you can put it in the very worst of places: stuff it under the mattress or into one of those fake soup cans. You can stash it in a hollowed-out book on the den shelf. Sure it's O.K. to keep a few bucks in the dwelling — gives a certain sense of security, I keep a few bucks in a dictionary in the "c" section for "currency" — but having any significant amount of dough stored in the house, or in a safety deposit box, is imprudent...no, make that dumb.

Who needs cash anymore? We're almost a cashless society now. You can gas up the family buggy, buy about anything at stores, get prescriptions filled, make phone calls, pay tolls, even use vending machines without having a greenback pass through your hands. I recently flew to Los Angeles. The airline ticket, the meal at the terminal, the rental car, the hotel were all paid with plastic. Paper money and coins of the realm are fast becoming obsolete...future collectors' items.

While offering some financial advice, this chapter's main purpose is to impress the reader with its concern about how money is so strongly related to contextica. Let's examine a few related recommendations.

### *Home, Sweet Home*

First, *the best contextica for your money is purchasing a home*. It is the biggest asset most of us have. I just finished reading a best seller on financial advice in which the author maintained that owning a home was *not* a good investment! *Wrong, wrong, wrong!* Here are four cogent reasons why he's all wet...or at least somewhat damp...on that.

1. "Everybody's gotta be someplace." That old Myron Cohen punch line reminds us that shelter is one of our most basic needs. Everybody — except the homeless — needs a roof over their heads. You can't live in a stock certificate or a savings account.

2. Paying on a home mortgage forces one to salt away some money each month. We're not a

thrift-conscious country anymore. Japan's savings rate quintuples ours so that any amount we can sock away is to our benefit.

3. Our homes give us unique breaks with the Internal Revenue Service. There are few deductions left in our federal tax code so we ought to take full advantage of the ones that remain. To encourage home ownership, Uncle Sam allows breaks for property taxes and interest on home loans. Also, when you sell your home, much if not all of the profit (capital gain) is exempt from taxation. That's a big one.

4. Appreciation of the value of your home can make you rich or, at least, add a great deal to your wealth. Residences in the Bay Ridge section of Brooklyn, New York have doubled in value in just the last five years! That's not an isolated case as most areas in the United States have experienced significant appreciation for the last several decades. Contrary to what the author previously referred to says — "homes are not a good investment because of low or no inflation" — the increases have held true even though the last several years have been ones of very low inflation rates. The purchase of a home has been, is, and will be one of the very best of places for your money. Keep in mind an appreciation of appreciation.

The economic law of supply and demand has not been rescinded. The population of the United States (demand) has doubled in the last seventy-five years but the land (supply) has remained the same. In the near and far future our population will continue to burgeon with everyone needing a place to hang their hats, but there will be no new land, except for new acreage like that being created by the Mississippi River at its delta. This is also true on a global basis. With over a threefold increase in the last three score and ten years, the size of our planet stubbornly remains the same.

Check the prices of land lots in your neighborhood today with what they were a decade ago. I'd be surprised if you or someone you know hasn't said: "I coulda bought that place a few years ago for a song ($80,000). It just sold like a symphony ($250,000).

A New York tycoon was asked for his secret of success in amassing his huge fortune. His response was that all through his life he *bought* real estate properties but he never *sold* any. Judicious purchases, good management and the gift of appreciation with time resulted in his spectacular wealth.

All right, so you may not be interested in becoming a real estate magnate. I would still like to belabor the point that home ownership is a good deal for you. Review your own experience with buying a house or houses. If you're a young reader, look at the homes your parents or grandparents have owned. I'll bet the family farm (don't own one, so you'll never collect if you win) that those properties are now worth a bundle more. There may be rare exceptions where neighborhoods have gone radically down because of pollution, land poisoning or escalating crime rates. Even then, the force of appreciation may prevail. The Office of Federal Housing Enterprising Oversight reported that the average (which included all price ranges) house nationwide *gained 34.8% in the four-year period from 1996 to 2000.*

**Keep in mind an appreciation of appreciation.**

A personal example. My father built rows of beautiful brick bungalows in the early thirties in Chicago which sold new for $3000. Non-hospital births were common then and I was born in one of those houses. I revisited my birthplace a few years ago. The neighborhood had undergone many changes and is now inhabited by a mix of homeowners and renters of low socioeconomic status. With high crime plaguing the area the houses are, nevertheless, selling in the $60,000. range — a twenty fold appreciation!

As to the "no inflation, no appreciation" argument. Come on, there has always been inflation. Only the rate or amount varies. Years of real deflation in our history are almost nonexistent. Look at the long-term graph of the Dow Jones stocks indicator. Look at what a movie theater ticket, hotel room or college tuition would cost just a few years ago as compared to today. My first brand new automobile was a '56 Dodge for which I paid the handsome sum of $3800. I'm getting ready to buy a new Toyota Prius — the one with the hybrid engine — which will probably cost around $24,000. That's less than the average amount new car buyers are shelling out for their sets of wheels. Yes, the cars today are more technologically advanced, but you get the idea. Inflation has been, is now and will be with us as a fact of life. We should use it to our advantage.

Another personal example — I said I was going to belabor this — is the case of our first born son, Richard, a writer-producer of science fiction in Los Angeles. He and his wife purchased a little home in an older but well-kept section of the city. The house — located near the La Brea Tar Pits Museum — was over 60 years old and in need of major repairs. I thought the asking price of $225,000 was absurd but the real estate market in California then was so hot that people were snatching up homes as soon as they were on the market. They bought the place and it *doubled* in value in just three years. That was then, and this is now, you say? The *Los Angeles Daily News* reported in December 2000 that home prices in the San Fernando area were continuing to soar at an annual rate of 19.5 percent.

And yet another personal example and the last on this topic. Our other son, Rob and his wife, Jody purchased an older home in Eden Prairie, Minnesota, where he works for a television sales company. A rambling ranch-style house situated on one of the state's zillion lakes, it also needed some TLC. They bought it in 1995 for $137,000. With re-roofing and some kitchen modernization, they have approximately $150,000 committed to it. Based on recent comparable sales in the neighborhood, they are confident it could easily sell for over $200,000 today.

Both sons reap the benefits of what is termed *leverage*. Both bought their homes with 20 percent down payments using mortgages of 80 percent. All of the appreciated value, however, goes to the homeowner and none to the lender. There is no 20-80 split of the enhanced value of the property. That is leverage...using the mortgagee's (the bank's) money to make money for you.

Let's say Rob and Jody sold their house now for $200,000. Their cost price for the property was $150,000 (purchase price plus costs of improvement). You might say they made $50,000 on the deal for a 33 percent profit. Not bad, but wrong. Remember they only put up 20 percent of the purchase or $27,400. That amount plus the improvements of approximately 13 grand puts their total investment at $40,400. That would represent a five-year rate of return on their home sale of a *whopping 80 percent!*

"Wait . . . there's more!" — as those television sales commercials like to say. "If you order today, you'll also get . . . " The more in this case is that Jody and Rob, in selling their house, would not have to pay one penny to Uncle Sam for their capital gains. In 1995 most profits from the sale of personal residences were exempted from federal income tax. The fifty thou would be *all* theirs.

If home ownership is a financially rewarding context for your money, then the more expensive the property, the greater the reward possibilities. Buy the highest price property you can get commensurate with your needs and your ability to make the payments. Celebrities like Cher, Gloria Estefan, Kenny Rogers and Madonna have purchased multimillion dollar residences on the east and west coasts and then sold them a few years later for millions more than their original costs. Ah, yes — the rich do get richer.

For every $100,000 of value in real estate — assuming a very conservative appreciation rate of just three percent — it becomes $103,000 after the first year. Property in the United States has consistently appreciated annually between one and twenty percent for the last several decades. The rate, of course, is dependent upon the particular locale. In some places values have skyrocketed beyond the twenty percent while in other areas, they've remained relatively stable. Checking with a local real estate broker will tell you what the story is in your neck of the woods. Again, assuming that the $100,000 represents $20,000 of your money and $80,000 from a mortgage, look what happens after just five years. (Incidentally, I would never buy with less than twenty percent down. If I did, the mortgagee will require I pay a monthly insurance fee in which the lender is the sole beneficiary should I default on the note.)

After year one . . . . $100,000 inflates to $103,000.
After year two . . . $103,000 increases to $106,090.
After year three . . $106,090 goes to $109,273.

After year four . . . $109,273 enlarges to $112,551.

After year five . . . $112,551 becomes $115,928.

The Bottom Line: That's a near $16,000 appreciation — an 80 percent gain on the $20,000 investment — accrued . . . *even while sleeping!*

### *Get Out of Town*

Although the gains don't come close to matching those accruing from real estate ownership, money kept in checking, savings, money market and certificates of deposit accounts are certainly good safe contexts for it. They are more liquid than real estate and we like that security of knowing that we can get cash very quickly. The ubiquitous presence of automatic teller machines lends credence to the only slightly exaggerated observation that "in America, there is cash on every street corner." We can draw out hundreds from any of those accounts in seconds from an ATM located in the nearby shopping center. Even while traveling we have instant access to our funds in airports, hotels, shopping malls, cruise ships, casinos . . . just about anywhere.

Having and building savings in those contexts can enable the purchase of a home, or, if that's been done, to then consider investing in stocks and/or bonds after a certain cushion level has been reached. We'll talk more about equity investments later in the chapter. For now let's agree that it's good to have some money in the bank.

There should be enough in an interest-bearing checking account to cover monthly bills and expenses but not more than is needed. If you carry a large balance in checking month after month, you're throwing money away. Money market funds offer better interest than checking accounts (generally true) but not as much as certificates of deposit. CD's offer the best rates but there are penalties for early withdrawals. Regardless of which product (that's what financial institutions call them) or products you use, you should of course seek out the best rate of return possible. To attain that, you may have to get out of town.

### *"Local People Serving Local People"*

That used to be the advertising slogan of a large national financial institution. It had just bought out a small town's little home-grown bank and was cleverly trying to convince depositors that it was still staffed by the local gentry and not by carpetbaggers. In reality, there are very few truly local banks anymore. Mergers and acquisitions have drastically reduced their number to near extinction. The friendly banker, who knew every depositor's name, portrayed in *It's a Wonderful Life* has gone the way of doctors who make house calls. Federal regulations have eased in the last decade. Now financial institutions can do more business across state lines and this has been a boon to the private investor because it has made for greater competition. Rarely does a month go by that the mailbox doesn't have an invitation from an out-of-state credit-card company offering their best deal. They're all working furiously to get your deposits or to lend you money or both. That puts you in the driver's seat, but you have to take the right road to then get to where you want to go and there are plenty of road maps available. Getting the best context for your savings may involve going beyond the nine dots of your immediate area.

Let's say Dudley DoWrong got out of his credit-card debt and amassed $5,000 to put into savings. He goes to the bank that has his checking account and gets a certificate of deposit for one year at 5.35 percent, compounded quarterly. At the end of the year his five thou has blossomed to $5,273. Not bad. Could he have done better? Absolutely.

Rachel Wise searched for the best rate she could get for a like amount of money. She didn't feel she had to deal with her bank but instead fired up her Hewlett-Packard and moused her way to the highest 1-year CD rates in her locale, in her state and in the entire United States. Typing in "Best Savings Deals Nationwide for 1 yr CD" elicited a 7 percent rate, compounded daily by a bank in Wilmington, Delaware. She verified the information by a provided toll-free call and verified the rate and the method of purchase of the certificate. A year later, she was enriched by $362 of interest compared to Dudley's $273. She got $89 more for the same principal amount invested for the same period of time and with the same FDIC protection.

**Getting the best context for your savings may mean going beyond the nine dots.**

Searching cyberspace for the highest-paying CD will yield at least one and perhaps even two higher percentage points than the typical CD offering. On the web, you can locate not only traditional banks but also those that offer CDs directly online. They can be very competitive because doing business online is cheaper than operating and staffing a branch office. They also know that customers need an incentive to venture into cyberspace. Nonetheless, many are still reluctant to take advantage of buying via the computer. This will change as more and more people become computer literate. Once automatic teller machines were adjudged safe, they have become omnipresent.

If you're not into the computer world yet, again, what are you waiting for? You're now in the minority as over half of American adults have regular access to the

Internet. But if you're not, the same information is printed in many of the larger circulation newspapers. The *Wall Street Journal* each weekday lists the five highest payers of: Money Market Investments, One Month CDs, Two Month CDs, Six Month's CDs, One Year CDs, and Five Year CDS.

**Why not get the very best deal possible?**

Every Sunday the *New York Times* publishes the three highest payers of money market and CD accounts. As just one example: the March 4, 2001 edition listed a bank in California as paying 6 percent for a money market account while the national average for such deposits was 2.04 percent. That's almost a 4 percent difference! Albeit an exceptional variation, but you can usually find a full percentage or more advantage if you do a little shopping.

Why not get the best deal possible? This entails ridding ourselves of the notion that we must do business in the immediate area. State boundaries in the financial sense don't exist anymore. Just as you can drive the interstate highways irrespective of state lines, so also can you invest in any other city or state — any other context — which will give you the biggest bang for your bucks. To do otherwise is really cheating yourself.

### *Buy Low, Sell High*

In our continuing mission to emphasize the importance of contextica in our lives and, in this chapter, to our financial well being let's now look at the stock market as a place for your hard-earned shekels. Owning real estate, as I hope has been demonstrated, is a pretty safe investment and can be very profitable in the short and the long term. Savings in the form of money markets and certificates of deposit are sure things in that you will be enriched without any risk involved, given the blessing of the FDIC. The mere passage of time enhances our investments in both of those venues.

But if you want to get rich, according to many money gurus, the stock market is the way to go. All you have to do is buy low and sell high. Simple. You do enter into a riskier area, however. Although over the long haul the Dow Jones and other measures of the market have shown very healthy gains over the last several decades — since 1926 the average annual return on stocks was a very nice 11.35 percent — there is a tradeoff. The market is risky. It has its ups and downs although you wouldn't know it if you were just looking at the last decade of the 20$^{th}$ century. In the 1990's equities in all the major American stock markets collectively enjoyed a space shuttle ascent never before seen in economic history. Millions of people — many not much past the voting age — became millionaires. A lot of that money flowed into the purchase of lavish homes, luxury automobiles, magnificent yachts and extravagant vacations which further fueled the economy and resulted in even greater investor confidence. In defiance of the gravitational law that "what goes up must come down" and the prevailing economic theory of boom and bust cycles, we continued to invest bullishly as if the figurative bear was an extinct species. Companies, especially in the technological field, that made no profit were bid up to nonsensical levels. Something had to happen . . . and it did.

The new century began with the supposedly deceased bear charging back into the market with a vengeance. Portfolios built with marginal financing were wiped out and others were decimated mercilessly. Here's just one of many, many horror stories.

Jean Paul Campe is a Toronto businessman and poker-playing friend of mine. In 1996 he invested $5000 in a Japanese company called Softbank. The company is a large holding institution which has stakes in many of the world's cyber-corporations like Yahoo. At the height of the great bull market of the 90's, his stock — purchased at $80 per share — had grown sixteen-fold to over $1300 per share. His $5000 had mushroomed to $82,000 in just three years! He was going to cash out and pay a mortgage off but he didn't. Caught in the euphoria of the longest bull run in history, he — like many of us — held on thinking the mountain top was still to be reached. His holding is now worth considerably less than his original investment. What then can be said about equities as a good context for your money?

As one who has been knocked down, but not out, by the crash of 2001, I still believe the stock market can be a money tree, and I'll go out on one of its limbs and tell you why. First a caveat. After one has a substantial equity in a home and a tidy sum in savings (money market, CD's, Treasury notes, etc.), only then should *some* funds go into the market. How much? Never more than one can lose without such a loss affecting having bread on the table or worrying if the lights will be turned off.

Having said that, let me proffer six suggestions for venturing into stocks. They *can* be an excellent context for your hard-gotten dollars in that you could become very wealthy. I'm not a financial guru but my advice is based on decades of experience, reading extensively, attending seminars and — most importantly — learning from that taskmaster of all taskmasters . . . the "school of hard knocks."

1. Open an account with an online broker. Start small with, say, a thousand dollars until you become familiar with and confident about trading on the Internet. Buying and selling stocks on the computer has revolutionized the stock market giving the small investor the same resources as the big players and portfolio managers. You can get advice, research, past performance charts and news through your cyber-connection. *E-Trade* and *Ameritrade* are two of the leading brokers who will buy or sell stocks for you at nominal commissions and in lots less than a hundred. Those and many other firms offer research tools, real-time quotes, up-to-the-minute account statements and many other services.

Trading on the computer is easy after you understand the basic types of orders and how to execute them. The market order is one in which the broker buys (or sells) a stock for you at the price then being quoted on the exchange. A limit order is used when the price of a stock may be volatile and the purchaser wants to buy (or sell) the stock at a fixed amount. Limit orders cost a few dollars more than market orders but they shield from the risk of paying (or losing) more than one wishes in a fluctuating situation.

2. Consider buying mutual stock funds. These are safer for the neophyte investor. When you buy into a mutual fund, you are investing into a large and diversified portfolio of stocks. You gain the expertise of the fund manager whose job it is to ensure profits for the investors with a minimum of risk. The day-to-day performance of mutuals is generally much less volatile compared to individual stocks. Most funds allow small periodic investments which encourage savings and give the advantage of dollar cost-averaging. That last-mentioned strategy means regularly buying a stock or a mutual. When doing that, if the price of a stock (or mutual) goes down, the average cost of all those purchases is lowered. If the price rises, then more of that stock is in your possession.

3. If you buy individual stocks, *buy what you use*. A mutual fund or funds is a good way to go but you may want to have a little portfolio of your own choices. It's riskier but can be more profitable — and it's fun. Of course that fun part is when the stock is rising. When it's going south, don't fret. Give it time and if it doesn't recover, take your licks with a smile . . . or, at least, don't cry.

4. Have confidence in the long-term prosperity of our economy. If you believe — as I do — that America will continue to lead the world in business and technology for the foreseeable future and that our gross national product will gain each year, then that will be reflected in the stock markets. Sure, there will be dips and corrections along the way but the overall trend will be constantly upward. Use a context for your money which will go up with it.

5. Avoid day trading, options and buying on margin. Leave that to the high rollers. Yes, big money can be made in those endeavors but the odds are heavily against you.

Day trading — going in and out of stocks on a daily or weekly basis — can be hazardous to your health. Greg Millman's *Day Traders* recounts the stories of several day traders who lost their life's savings and some who have attempted suicide. It's been estimated that even in the halcyon days of the raging bull market of the previous decade, 70 percent of day traders lost their outer garments.

Options are instruments whereby one does not actually purchase a stock, but instead buys a right to perhaps buy that stock at a later date. The purchaser of an option gambles that the stock will go up in which case he will then buy that stock at the preset lower price, garnering a handsome profit. If the price does not go up, the option will not be exercised and the loss will just be the cost of buying that option.

Margin buying is the practice of buying stocks with money borrowed from a broker. The broker will do this because he has the security of holding the investor's portfolio as collateral. Brokers may allow purchases of 50 percent more than the cash value of the stocks one has. Interest is usually charged. In a worst case scenario, if our Dudley DoWrong were to borrow the maximum half of his portfolio's worth and put it all into a new stock and the stock flamed out, this would happen. The broker would then own Dudley's remaining portfolio. The broker would have collected interest on the margin loan and pocketed any commissions for the purchase and sale of the stock. Dudley — as a stock investor — would, of course, be broke

6. Stay away from the stock market if you're: nervous, anxious, excitable, prone to heart attacks, highly emotional, insecure and unable to handle disappointment. You're better off using the much safer money contexts of traditional savings instruments and real estate. Peace of mind, mental health are worth more than all the money in Marc Rich's Swiss bank accounts.

### *Loose Ends*

Before we close this — admittedly limited — discourse on money contextica, mention should be made of two other possibilities: IRAs and bonds.

To encourage saving for retirement, Uncle Sam wisely approved the setting up of Individual Retirement Accounts many decades ago. Since then the plan has been liberalized to allow for other goals such as paying for a first home or to pay for college costs for yourself, your kids or your grandchildren. One can invest up to $2000 per year and have income tax deferred or, in the case of a Roth IRA, not pay any federal income tax. Now, money can even be withdrawn — without penalty — for major medical expenses that exceed 7.5 percent of one's Adjusted Gross Income. It really pays to invest in an IRA. Consider this. If you open an IRA today and put in $2000 per annum for the next thirty years, your account will have grown — yes, even while you were sleeping — to a princely $329,000! That's before taxes and assuming a 10 percent return with no withdrawals. Enough to buy a reasonably priced small yacht equipped with a state-of-the-art computer.

Bonds are issued by corporations and governments to raise money. There is a promise to repay at a future date — usually one year or longer — and interest is paid during the term. Bonds are considered conservative investments not nearly as risky as stocks. One widely respected financial expert, Charles B. Carlson, says: "You get rich buying stocks. You stay rich buying bonds." Proof of that can be found in the case of Monica Seles. The one-time top female player in the world, whose career was critically interrupted by the senseless backstabbing in Germany, has amassed over 40 million from tennis, commercials and wise investments. A believer in real estate, she owns three homes. Her other assets are large holdings in stocks and in bonds. During a recent interview for an article in a financial magazine, she "confided" to the writer that, although her stock holdings were down, income from her bonds would yield over $400,000 a year for her. Not too shabby.

> **"You get rich buying stocks. You stay rich buying bonds.**

Let's go from riches to rags. Our frugal Rachel Wise accepts spendthrift Dudley DoWrong's proposal of marriage. (Do financial opposites attract?) They're in their late twenties, both work. Dudley's in debt up to his receding hair line while Rachel has a little over $8,000 in her checking account and a certificate of deposit. She also has a $4,000 IRA. Her car, a 1999 Toyota, is free and clear. Dudley pays $240 a month on a note for his 1998 Corvette which has a balance of $9,000.
They had both rented but after the nuptials, Dudley moved to her apartment. (I know what you're thinking: "Why, on earth, did she marry this guy?")

Let's assume Rachel Wise and Dudley DoWrong apply the **Four Steps** plan of Chapter Five to the contextica of their finances. It could go something like this . . .

***Self Analysis:*** What is our net worth? What are our assets, liabilities?
Are we too much in debt?
Are we getting the best return on our investments?
Is our income"as good as it gets?"
What do our near-future earnings look like?
What do we want out of life?

***Set Goals:*** To be free of debt and save enough money to make a down payment on the purchase of a home in two years.

***Self Start:*** Cut up all credit cards except one. Both agree to use the one card for all agreed-upon purchases.
Adhere to an austere program which would include: selling the Corvette and making do with one car; brown-bagging lunches four of five workdays; dining out just once a month; renting movies more often rather than paying admission prices; Dudley getting an extra part-time job while Rachel agrees to work more hours at her firm; immediately banking a set amount from both paychecks as they are received.

***Succeed:*** In two years the couple is debt-free and have money for a d.p.!

Dudley and Rachel are to be commended. They worked together to examine where they were financially in the ***Self Analysis*** and then ***Set Goals*** which were realistic and achievable. They ***Self Start***ed by brainstorming as to how to attain the goals using the checklist as a guide. (*Eliminate* some credit cards and one car, *Combine* assets and debts, *Magnify* income from *Expanded* work schedules, *Minimize* expenses for movies and dinners.) They Succeeded by evaluating that they had reached their goals. They could now begin to look for the home of their dreams and start thinking about new aspirations.

Summarizing this chapter, I've urged that owning a home is a great context for your money, as are regular savings in the form of money markets, CDS and IRAs. For those with a suitable financial base and the right temperament, there are fortunes to be made (or lost) in the stock market. And if you're one who profits handsomely in the equities market, then stash a lot into bonds.

Bad debt was differentiated from good debt. Bad debt in the form of carrying large credit card balances habitually is — ( "stupid" was used before) — idiotic. Also beware of those ads inviting you to get a loan on the equity you have in your home. They are second mortgages. Some trumpet lending based on 125 percent of the market value of your house, so eager are they to get your lucrative business. Unfortunately, Uncle Sam has been their partner in crime. For some puzzling reason IRS allows interest paid on home equity loans to be tax deductible while other loans are not. If you need $20,000 to buy a new car and you get it from a second mortgage on your castle, the interest you pay can be listed on your Schedule D. But if you finance the twenty G's through GMAC, it is not. Thus, our beloved uncle — who is so good to homeowners in the ways we've cited — now encourages lessening your equity in the house. If you *really* need the money (the new car) and if the interest rate is the best you can get (factoring in the income tax aspect), then going the equity loan route may be justified and thought of as good debt. If you do, try to pay it off as soon as you can.

**Carrying large credit card balances is idiotic.**

Put your money in the best places you can find. Never have there been greater opportunities to be so well informed as to where they are. Remember to remember Ben's age-old wisdom that:

(Another bottom line)

**TIME = $**

## Chapter Ten

# PUTTING IT ALL IN THE PROPER (you guessed it) CONTEXT

This final chapter will have two parts. The first will be a (yipes!) TEST. As a former teacher I feel an obligation to have you check on yourselves as to how much you've remembered from the foregoing pages. Don't worry, you'll all do just fine. I'm sure you'll belie the assertions that we Americans have an attention span of about twenty minutes and that we forget ninety-five percent of what we read in a couple of hours.

I've always liked the *Reader's Digest*'s "It Pays to Improve Your Word Power" because they give the answers conveniently on the next page. But I'm not going to do that. This is a really tough test! There will be no answers given. It's an open book exam, however, so you can feel free to peruse the pages. I doubt that will be necessary once you get my (wink) drift.

The second part will be a mishmash of afterthoughts, updates, amplifications, remarks, footnotes and other miscellany which either did not quite fit into the chapters or had not come to my attention until later. We'll conclude this concluding chapter with a summary of the most important points in the book, which I hope and pray will be etched in your memory, chiseled into your mind, and adapted into your daily actions.

Most do-it-yourselfers have a tray or jar in which they toss various nails, screws, nuts and bolts, fasteners, etc. Crafts people have their baskets of bits, scraps and remains from other projects. Both know the value of not throwing stuff away. I have file folders filled with articles, references, cartoons, photographs and other materials which I kept because I thought they would be of use some day. Well, today is that day. Much of the mishmash goes into these last pages.

But first . . .

## THE TEST

Directions: Select the *one* best answer. There may be two, or even three, best answers but you may select just one. Add the correct responses (you'll know which are correct) and see how well you've done at the end of the test.

1. Of approximately six billion earthlings, each is different because of:
   a. our social security numbers.
   b. our waist measurements.
   c. *where* we are and the *times* we live in.

2. "Contextica" means:
   a. a continuous index.
   b. words of a convict.
   c. one's place and time.

3. When in Rome we do, indeed, become:
   a. agitated.
   b. Greeks.
   c. Romans.

4. The interplay of nature and nurture determines:
   a. the outcome of the World Series.
   b. the rise and fall of the stock market.
   c. who we are.

5. Walk up to the next person you see with a great big smile on your face and:
   a. she'll think you're an idiot.
   b. he'll wonder if he left his fly open.
   c. he or she will probably also smile.

6. The Robin Cook referred to in this book is:
   a. England's former foreign minister.
   b. a world-famous chef.
   c. a creative contexter.

7. Mitzi Ross found her mate by:
   a. offering a dowry.
   b. corresponding with a prison inmate.
   c. intentionally being in the right place at the right time.

8. You never can swim in the same river twice because:
   a. it has become polluted.
   b. you got tired the first time.
   c. everything is constantly changing.

9. The "Nine Dots" represents:
   a. a vision screening test.
   b. a top view of nine posts.
   c. a reminder that we should go beyond our imagined limits.

10. "Activated Catenated Psychosynapsis" means:
   a. cats lead active lives.
   b. cats lead crazy lives.
   c. thinking . . . moving messages around in the brain.

11. If Archimedes, Shakespeare, Pasteur, Salk and Einstein had television in their days:

a. they would all have been stars on the Discovery Channel.
b. their spouses would have fought for the remote.
c. we'd probably still be in the dark ages

.

12. Motivation comes from:

a. a nagging spouse.
b. Pittsburgh.
c. within ourselves.

13. One of the prime elements of human uniqueness is:

a. belching.
b. having ear lobes.
c. the ability to create and exercise new options.

14. "Ideational Fluency" is:

a. usually accompanied by fever and nausea.
b. never accompanied by fever and nausea.
c. coming up with as many ideas as one can on a problem or topic.

15. A mnemonic device refers to:

a. a medieval torture machine.
b. a money changer.
c. remembering something by associating it with something else.

16. "Checklisting" is:

a. numerically organizing checks.
b. a description of an inebriated citizen of the Czech Republic.
c. a useful technique for problem solving by applying a list in the solution-finding process.

17. "Forced Relationships" refers to:
  a. blind dates.
  b. having in-laws.
  c. creating ideas by combining seemingly unrelated things.

18. "Morphological Analysis" has to do with:
  a. an autopsy.
  b. Greek mythology.
  c. an organized way of forcing relationships in idea-finding by using two or three-dimensional matrices.

19. "Free Association" means:
  a. you can join without paying any admission charges.
  b. the name of a company founded by Jefferson Free.
  c. activated catenated psychosynapsis, musing, thinking, contemplating.

20. The "pleasure-pain" concept refers to:
  a. a cult of sadomasochists.
  b. visiting the dentist.
  c. the human tendency to be drawn to pleasureful contexts and to avoid or withdraw from painful situations.

21. In relation to the context of time for enrolling children in school, the book:
  a. suggests arriving early for registration.
  b. warns about head lice.
  c. strongly recommends ensuring that a child have the advantage of being among the older rather than younger classmates.

22. Barbara and Lou Krane's use of a matrix to help in deciding where to retire resulted in their choice of:

a. Antarctica.
b. Iraq.
c. Florida.

23. "Now" is:

a. the name of a national organization.
b. the admonition a parent gives to a child.
c. the best of all times.

24. Not since the Biblical era has it been so hazardous to:

a. drive on city streets.
b. eat apples.
c. make physical love.

25. There is now a thin line between:

a. North and South Carolina.
b. solvency and bankruptcy.
c. honest courting and sexual harassment.

26. The measurement of time began:

a. when the boss observed your arrival at work.
b. after the first yardstick was invented.
c. about 4,000 years ago.

27. One of the best ways to lose weight is:

a. amputation.
b. donating blood.
c. eating nothing after 3:00 P.M.

28. The <u>most important thing</u> you and I have is:

a. the remote for the TV.

b. the remote for the garage door opener.

c. time.

29. The fewest marriages and divorces occur:

a. in polygamous unions.

b. in Pittsburgh.

c. during the month of January.

30. The story about filling the jar with rocks, gravel, sand and water demonstrates the importance of:

a. never doing today what can be put off until tomorrow.

b. avoiding drinking while driving.

c. prioritizing your goals.

31. Never buy stocks:

a. period.

b. with counterfeit money.

c. before a long weekend.

32. While you are sleeping:

a. use a nose patch to avoid snoring.

b. blood pressure spikes up.

c. your financial position is getting better or worse.

33. The best context for your money is:

a. in a can buried in the back yard.

b. casinos.

c. the purchase of a home.

34. Inflation is:
    a. what happens to our waist lines after 40.
    b. a fisherman's measurement of his catch.
    c. an economic fact of life.

35. Leverage is:
    a. an expensive French perfume.
    b. not to be confused with road rage.
    c. using the lender's money to take advantage of appreciation for your gain.

36. You get rich buying stocks . . . you stay rich:
    a. never spending anything.
    b. by saying "no" to your relatives.
    c. buying bonds.

37. Convergent and divergent thinking:
    a. can cause severe headaches.
    b. has been banned in Congressional debates.
    c. are two sides of the same coin; they complement each other.

38. Anything we can imagine:
    a. should be kept quiet.
    b. is forgivable.
    c. we can accomplish.

39. Ray Kroc, the founder of McDonald's, thought that the most important trait to consider in a candidate for employment was:
    a. height.
    b. a love of hamburgers.
    c. motivation.

40. The man who encountered the street sign which read "One Way Only" stopped and proceeded in the opposite direction. He then realized:
   a. he was on the wrong street.
   b. he left his wallet at home.
   c. he was on foot.

41. All English literature ever written:
   a. was plagiarized from France.
   b. has been translated from Hebrew.
   c. is simply differing arrangements of the twenty-six letters of our alphabet.

42. The four steps suggested as an aid to creatively contexting your life:
   a. were developed by Fred Astaire and Arthur Murray.
   b. included: "One for the money, two for the show, three to get ready, four to go."
   c. were *Self Analysis, Set Goals, Self Start, Succeed.*

43. One of the major theses of this book is that you:
   a. should brush your teeth twice a day.
   b. never brush your teeth so as to prevent damage to the gums.
   c. set aside time for regular ***sessions with yourself*** to think about your contextica.

44. Consider a goal as:
   a. a misspelling of "ghoul."
   b. the horizontal pole suspended between two upright posts.
   c. a contract with yourself.

45. Thinking has a tendency to be:
   a. upsetting to your stomach.
   b. strengthened by a rigorous diet of fish food.
   c. unfocused, vague and easily distracted.

46. A tipping point is reached:

a. when the meal is finished.
b. on the last day of a cruise.
c. when the painful aspects of a situation conclusively override the pleasureful aspects (or the reverse) finally causing a change in behavior.

47. Creative thinking ability is innate in:

a. artists, composers, architects and politicians — exclusively.
b. rabbits.
c. each and every one of us.

***

Almost finished . . . just three more to go. You've worked hard. It's time for a well-deserved break..........................................................................................................

..........................................................................................................

..........................................................................................................

.....................................*signifies break* ....................................................................

..........................................................................................................

***

48. The New York City chef who warned never to order fish in a restaurant on Mondays reasoned that:

a. menu prices are highest at the beginning of the week.
b. it's a good night to stay home and watch the *Monday Nite Movie.*
c. the fish may be several days old.

49. You are who you are because:

a. of a sensible diet.
b. we were victorious in World War II.
c. of your interaction with your *contextica* (environment and time).

50. Throughout the book, you are urged to regularly ask yourself:

a. have I flossed my teeth today?

b. should I choose paper or plastic shopping bags?

c. ***where am I, and what time is it ?***

All right. That concludes that tough test (whew!). Congratulations are in order, I'm sure. I know you got all fifty questions answered correctly. If you didn't, ask for a refund (fat chance) for the book. Yes, some items did have more than one correct answer. In question 13, for instance, "having ear lobes" is also a unique characteristic of humans. But let us not quibble. The purpose of THE TEST, of course, was to summarize — in a light vein emulating a little of Dave Barry's inimitable style — some of the serious major points of the book.

And now these final pages will include a mishmash of topics related to contextica and they're in no particular order. The topics didn't quite fit in any of the chapters, but they are pertinent to a further appreciation of the importance of time and place to all aspects of our behavior.

## Contextica and Humor

Another attribute which is unique to the human condition is our ability to laugh, chuckle or grin at something funny . . . to have a sense of humor. How dismal a world this would be without mirth. But what is this phenomenon? What is humor anyway? Dr. Sid Parnes defined it as the stuff of "logical incongruities." The dictionary describes it as "a comic or absurd quality causing amusement." Dave Barry writes articles and books and won a Pulitzer Prize for his consistent tickling of our funny bones. Norman Cousins credits laughter as a formidable ally in fighting cancer with no prescription necessary and no side effects. Rabbi-historian Joseph

Krizlov maintains that Jews have been able to survive centuries of discrimination and persecution partly because of the gift of humor. (Indeed, the vast majority of American comedians are from a Jewish heritage.)

Humor is the quintessential manifestation of creativity. We need: innovative solutions to old problems, inspiring art and music to enrich our lives, advanced technology to make us even more comfortable or to lengthen our tenure on this planet. But we also need to laugh to help us cope with "the slings and arrows of outrageous fortune." (As we know, Shakespeare was also a comedian.)

We can easily see how ideas for humor can come from using the creative techniques described in this book. Cartoonists rely heavily on forcing relationships or using some of the verbs from Osborn's check list. The execution scene ("Before we begin, have you heard the one about . . . ") depicted earlier is a hilarious example of forcing standup comedy with the role of the executioner. Magnifying (exaggeration) is a much relied upon tool for getting us to laugh.

**Humor depends upon contextica.**

Humor is critically dependent upon time and place. What may be hilarious in one contextica may be anathema in another. Fifty or so years ago people roared at the antics of Amos and Andy or at black-faced comedians in minstrel shows. Today, in a more sensitive society, such humor is absolutely taboo. Times change and humor along with it.

As another example, I'll tell you of a very embarrassing personal experience if you promise not to tell anyone. It was that humiliating.

It was at the first administrators' meeting of a school district in which I, as a newcomer, was being welcomed as a new principal appointee. Dr. John Lawson, the superintendent who went on to become one of Horace Mann's successors as Commissioner of Education for the Commonwealth of Massachusetts, directed that I tell a joke as this was the custom and a requirement for initiation into the group.

This was the story I told:

> The young kindergarten teacher accepted the offer of a textbook salesman who had visited the school to go for a ride in the country after school that day. They drove out several miles and then parked along side the rural road. They became passionate and made love. As they started motoring back, she began to cry lamenting that she had such guilt feelings that it would be difficult for her to face her pupils tomorrow for what she had done <u>twice</u> that day.
>
> "Twice!" he exclaimed. "What do you mean? We just did it once." She replied coyly, "Aren't we going to stop again on the way home?"

There were, as I recall, about twenty people in the group. One of them was the Director of Instruction, who would be my immediate superior. She grimaced at the finish of the punch line which aborted any further laughter from the few who started to chuckle. There was then an awkward silence during which I would have gladly crawled into that proverbial hole to escape what I now realized was a major faux pas. After the meeting, I apologized to the director as profusely as I could for my impropriety. She accepted it graciously and we worked together harmoniously for many years. When she retired, I assumed her position. Thank you, Miss McFarland . . . wherever you are.

To the extent that humor is dependent upon time and place, it is therefore risky. Much of it needs a victim and consequently there is always the danger of alienating someone. One of the most successful TV programs of the nineties, *Seinfeld*, was able to pull off jokes which could have angered many groups in an earlier time. There were shows about: handicapped people in wheelchairs, the "bubble boy," elderly retirees, masturbation, homosexuality, a gossiping rabbi and others which evoked mirth in millions when, in earlier times and in certain places, there would have been groans and grimaces. I know . . . been there, done that.

Look at this logical incongruity.

(Reprinted with permission of UNIVERSAL PRESS SYNDICATE.)

We can accept the logic of a large business looking to improve its product. But the basic paper clip has retained its original form and popularity through so many decades that tampering with it seems an absurd notion . . . an incongruity.

Of course the paper clip design *has* been changed many times — perhaps by using Osborne's check list. It has been *magnified* to the giant clip, *minified* to a tiny version, *combined* with color and has had metal *substituted* with plastic. Just about any object around you has been changed to its present form by having the italicized verbs applied.

Summarily, humor is dependent upon its contextica. Place and time determine whether it is laughable . . . or groanable. Conceiving comedy is a truly creative, but risky, endeavor. Let's close this section with a chuckle which typifies the cartoonist's clever use of the checklist tool of *reversal.*

## Contextica and Sociology

Our history is a record of continuous change of place — some voluntary, some forced. We can safely surmise that our primitive ancestors were constantly on the move going from one area to another in search of game or new vegetation in order to survive. This continues today when millions of people migrate from one country to another in search of a better way of life. Refugees risk their lives in crossing oceans and borders to escape poverty, danger or authoritarian governments. Jews fled Europe to escape religious persecution; hundreds of thousands of Irish migrated to shun the potato famine; Mexicans cross the Rio Grande daily to seek work in the good ole Estados Unidos. There are now 28.4 million immigrants living in the United States, the largest number ever in our nation's history.

Within our country, unending re-contexting has always been evident. The first colonists bred the pioneers who moved westward "from sea to shining sea" fulfilling our manifest destiny. In more modern times, Americans created cities, then moved to suburbs, then moved to the exurbs and rural areas. Southerners have migrated to the north and vice versa. A large part of our population changes locations every year.

An interesting example of a sociological change of context is the busing of school children in the United States during the last four decades to achieve racial integration. With a Supreme Court decision that ruled out the "separate, but equal" practices of school districts, many implemented programs of busing African-American pupils to previously white areas. The intent was to have students in classrooms which would more realistically reflect the nation's racial makeup. The exodus of white families to the suburbs and exurbs resulted in the resegregation of most large cities. That has led to a belief that meaningful integration of the races cannot be achieved by simply changing the school context alone. Housing patterns which represent diversity, will more effectively integrate the races.

During the last few years another sociological phenomenon, which has become a volatile issue nationally, is seen in the practice of racial or ethnic profiling. Police would stop and question black males because of their contextica: late night and in a high crime area. In the aftermath of the 9/11 tragedies, ethnic profiling techniques were used in an attempt to guard against terrorism by focusing attention on people who appeared to be of Arab descent. Some law enforcement authorities say the methods are necessary while others claim it is unfair stereotyping and civil rights are being violated.

What do you think?

## Contextica and Psychology

Our perceptions of reality are heavily influenced by context. Look at this. Which boy is the tallest?

You would swear (I would) that the lad at the top is the biggest of the three. He's not. All three are exactly the same size. Go ahead . . . get a ruler and check it out. Only their backgrounds (contexts) are different. The "tallest" one's head is above the roof of the adjoining building making the "shortest" boy whose head is below the roof seem dwarfish by comparison.

A room can be made to look larger than it is by painting it all one color rather than having the walls of one hue and the doors and trim work of another. Interior designers know that light colors tend to magnify spaces while dark do the opposite.

Think of all the restaurants you've been in where one or more of the walls have been mirrored, giving an impression of a much larger dining area.

Colors of the interior of a room can also influence moods, according to Rosemary Sadez Friedmann, a writer and professional member of the prestigious American Society of Interior Designers. Green, blue and black are soothing and tend to decrease blood pressure while red, orange and yellow do the opposite. She also reports that therapists use yellow surroundings to treat patients with arthritis, rheumatism, eczema, and constipation and choose orange contexts for asthma, colds, and thyroid problems. Don't know if I buy all that, but I do know that many prison death row walls are painted a mint green because of some research that indicated it was restful to the condemned inmates.

**Clothing manufacturers rely heavily on contextual persuasion.**

Clothing manufacturers rely heavily on contextual persuasion by designing apparel which seems to make one appear taller or shorter, heavier or leaner. Most men know that a single-breasted suit is preferable to a double-breasted outfit if height enhancement is the goal. Just about all women understand that solid black garments are slimming, while white or light-colored clothes are broadening. Horizontal stripe patterns emphasize wideness and being short. Vertical stripes accentuate thinness and tallness.

Humphrey Bogart, Alan Ladd, Frank Sinatra were just a few of actors who were usually deliberately cast with shorter co-stars so as not to appear short themselves. They also relied on apparel in the form of built-up footwear to appear taller. And, going to the other end of the body, how about all those stars who succeeded in having us perceive them as something they were not? I'm talking about the bald or nearly bald guys who presented themselves as hirstute heartthrobs always winning the hands of lovely leading ladies. Would Sean Connery, Burt Reynolds or Ted Danson have been the matinee idols they were without the benefit of their clever contextual accommodation of a toupee?

Maybe . . . maybe not.

Another interesting psychological aspect of context can be seen in the positioning of people when they're in small groups. If three individuals, who all work for the same company, are walking through a hallway at the office — the one in the middle will probably be the boss. Subordinates will flank the superordinate rather than take center stage, either consciously or subconsciously. If the same three go to dine, you can almost surely bet that the single-file line following the maitre d' will be headed by the higher honcho.

**One's grooming and clothing contexts can affect being hired or fired.**

In the work world, the psychological effects one's grooming and clothing contexts have on a job interviewer can be the difference between being hired or being told "don't call us, we'll call you." A recent (year 2000) survey of 1,756 bosses by the National Association of Colleges and Employers rated grooming as tops in making a favorable impression on recruiters. Nontraditional appearance — as in indiscreet clothing, weird hair color, tattoos, male earrings and body piercing — was considered a turnoff by over 70 percent of the respondents.

Human sexual behavior has always been closely tied to time and place. In some earlier primitive centuries and cultures, a woman committing adultery would have been stoned to death. Today, an admitted adulteress writes a book, for millions of bucks, about her affair and is an international celebrity. The sexual revolution begun by Dr. Kinsey continues to this day. Wow, how times have changed!

People in different places have various ideas about what constitutes sexual attractiveness. For centuries, Chinese males have lusted for women whose feet were bound from infancy so that they were the size of a small child's. The practice was outlawed many years ago but is documented at length in *The Art of Chinese Foot Binding*. In present day sub-Saharan Africa, men and women insert rings in their noses and stretch their necks so as to appear attractive to the opposite sex. In eighteenth century western Europe, the plump (full-figured) woman was the ideal sex partner as depicted in the art of Reuben and other masters of the era. Bare female breasts in Tahiti or Africa go without notice while American (and other) women undergo expensive surgery to enhance bust lines knowing Western-culture males will pay rapt attention.

Extremes in human nature? In some Muslim societies, females must be fully clothed except for the eyes. Anything less is considered vulgar. But on the beaches of the Riviera, men and women sun themselves wearing only . . . sun tan lotion.

Ah, yes . . . these wide variations of human behavior are what make the study of psychology so endlessly fascinating.

## Contextica and Philosophy

Our systems of beliefs guide our choices as to where we place ourselves and thus are very personal and subjective. Small towns and rural areas are not for free-love groups or transvestites who like to parade in public. Big cosmopolitan cities are more accepting of different life styles. If you're a staunch adherent of a certain religion, you surely want to be near the church of your choosing. This is a high priority. Some people like mountains, others hate them. Want peace and privacy? Look to rural America. Crave action? Las Vegas, with it's 24/7 glitz and gambling, beckons. (That city is currently the fastest growing area in the entire U.S.) Hate cold weather? Go south.

Time for a relevant joke break:

> Many years ago in a small town in the deep south, a Greyhound bus, en route from New York City, made a rest stop. Among the passengers was an orthodox rabbi who wore the traditional yarmulka and long black robe. His sideburn hair was long and braided as was/is the custom. The locals had never seen a clergyman like the rabbi and many curiously gaped at him as he was returning to the bus. Noticing the attention he was getting, the holy man turned to the spectators and good-naturedly asked: "What's the matter? You never seen a Yankee before?"

Our religious beliefs control much of our contextica. Churches, temples and synagogues mandate or strongly urge us to be in certain places at certain times; attend Mass on Sunday (or Saturday), go to the temple on Sabbath. Their moral codes also determine places we should not be (e.g., dens of iniquity, etc.). We long to be part of some community imbued with righteousness, purpose and direction. Without the world's great religions, where would civilization now be. Probably not very civilized.

**Without the world's great religions, where would civilization now be?**

Deepak Chopra gets right to the essence of our struggle to understand who we are, and why we are here as temporary inhabitants of this planet. He asks: "Are we spiritual beings having a physical experience . . . or are we physical beings having a spiritual experience?" Ah, that *is* the question.

Another bit of humor. I think this is one of the funniest (and deepest) ever. Although I've told it in dozens of classes, the response was always disappointing. Heard it from the late teacher-comedian Sam Levenson. Maybe you'll like it.

> Two fellows were philosophizing about life. One said: "Ya know Jake, with this world the way it is — all the crime and violence and poverty and the high taxes, diseases and the polluted air, and the threat of nuclear war — sometimes I think it's better never to have been born at all."
>
> "But," he continued, "who should be so lucky? Maybe one in a million!"

Glad I put two chuckles in before this last part which is definitely not a laughing matter — our *final contextica!*

## Contextica and Death

Who said: "Nothing is as certain as death; nothing as uncertain as its time and place?" Well, that may not be a valid statement any more as many would now like to set the time and place of their departure from this mortal coil. Enter Dr. Kevorkian, who is currently residing in jail because he complied with such wishes. His incarceration didn't end the debate about the right — if any — of an individual to leave this world when and where he or she should choose. The Netherlands recently passed a law allowing such choices. Indeed, one state — Oregon — has legitimized doctor-assisted suicide for the last several years. Other states vary in laws pertaining to keeping or removing life support systems. Not only do states differ, but so also do counties, hospitals and even doctors on these issues.

Religions and cultures strongly affect the "to be or not to be" question. For past generations of certain sects in India, the practice of "suttee" was followed. When the husband died, the grieving widow dutifully climbed up on the funeral pyre to be cremated with her mate.

Since the days of the Samurai warriors and continuing through World War II, the Japanese culture encouraged hara-kiri to atone for disgrace or to defend the homeland. Modern-day terrorists explode bombs strapped to their bodies or target highjacked jet planes to destroy buildings for religious or political ends. Roman Catholic theology forbids suicide, although if it is done in defense of the Church, it is termed martyrdom and sainthood may be conferred. Historically, Jews generally have disdained the taking of one's own life and the burial of suicides was often relegated to a crossroads site rather than the cemetery.

## The Tipping Point of Honey Alexander

During the last two years of Lamar Alexander's term of office as governor of Tennessee, he and his family made a momentous decision. They would make a very drastic change of context after he left office by moving to Australia for six months. At that time, in 1987, he was being talked about as a possible running mate for George Bush (the older one) and was also being urged by then-President Ronald Reagan to run for the Senate.

But during dinner one night in the governor's mansion, the first lady of the Volunteer State had reached a tipping point when she exclaimed to her husband, "We've got to get out of here." She felt that the family — they have four children — had drifted apart because of the time demands of the governorship and they needed to get together again. She also thought it would be good for him to think about what he wanted to do with the rest of his life.

They did move to Sydney and had the wonderful experience of strengthening the household which he describes in his book, *Six Months Off: An American Family's Australian Adventure.* When asked what was the most important lesson he learned from the move, he said: "I learned that I was glad I was married to someone who had enough gumption to suggest we do this while we still could." After their return, Lamar Alexander assumed the presidency of the University of Tennessee.

Honey's tipping point was reached at that dinner table, or some time just before, when she finally decided to broach the subject to her husband. Unfortunately, too many times, people never reach the position where there is a discernment that the situation is not satisfactory and that some kind of action needs to be taken. The pleasure-pain seesaw stays level. The tipping point never becomes a turning point. The critical mass doesn't quite attain enough force to set off a chain reaction. They procrastinate, saying "maybe tomorrow or next week." They should remember the words of Hubert Tinley: "Yesterday is a cancelled check. Tomorrow is a promissory note. Today is ready cash." We've reviewed some of the reasons: fear of change, apathy, staying in the rut, etc. The result of this kind of inaction is that many lead unhappy, unfulfilled lives. Pity, that.

## Three Score and Ten

Seventy years of life . . . that's it? Not according to a discernable trend reported in many articles. The fastest growing segment of the population in the vast majority of countries is the oldest of the old. In the United States, the 2000 census recorded 51,000 centenarians and it is projected that the number will increase to 324,000 by 2030. *The Futurist* (January 2000) suggests that persons born today could be living to age 100, caring for parents who are 140 and having their 70-year-old children living with them! If that does come about, and there is considerable evidence to support the contention, then our planet's population will increase even more dramatically. Ex-governor Lamm of Colorado was concerned about that when he proclaimed some time ago that it was the duty of old people — like those on life support systems — to die so as to make room on earth for the newborn. He never went on to higher political office.

In most countries, women live five to eight years longer than men. At the 85th year,females outnumber males by 2 to 1. Some attribute this difference to hormonal or genetic variations but others cite environmental factors. Men have historically placed themselves (or have been forced) into life-threatening pursuits. They are disproportionately represented in dangerous occupations such as the military, firefighters, police, race car and taxi drivers, airplane pilots (less than seven percent of licensed pilots in the United States are women), construction, bull-fighting, etc. Men tend to smoke and drink more. They drive faster, own more motorcycles, and see their doctors for physicals less than women. Gang murders and barroom brawl deaths are almost exclusively masculine events.Many more men than women commit suicide. Middle-aged males are four to five times more likely to kill themselves.

But whatever your age or gender, you can look forward to living a lot longer. Israel Haimowitz, was recently reported in an Associated Press article (Septmber 5, 2002 ) as having celebrated his hundreth birthday by renewing his driver's license.

Do we want to live to the triple-digit figure? A recent survey suggests most do not. Only 27 percent said they wanted to live to be a hundred. Reasons given were a fear of being in poor health and concern about having enough money to live on. If science can extend our time not only quantitavely but qualitatively as well, that would be a fantastic and wonderful development. I'd go for *two* hundred years.

## The Other Drug Culture . . . Us.

Do you know of anybody who doesn't take one or several pills or medications into their mouths on a daily basis? We regularly gulp vitamins, herbal supplements, pills to lose weight, pills to gain weight, antidepressants, capsules to thin blood, capsules to thicken blood, antihistamines, tablets to enhance sexual function, tablets to depress appetites, decongestants, drugs to get us to sleep and drugs to keep us awake. We are a pill-poppin' people.

Just about every visit to a doctor is followed by a trip to the pharmacy to pick up the prescription. Not only are "open 24 hours" pharmacy palaces sprouting up all over the country, but just about every Wal-Mart and supermarket boasts an apothecary on the premises. We Americans spend 122 billion dollars a year on drugs, according to the U.S. Dept. Of Health and Human Services. Drugstores are certainly everywhere in our environment. The availability and costs of drugs are national political issues and both parties try to outdo each other in their stances on the subject.

> **We Americans are a pill-poppin' people, spending 122 billion dollars a year on drugs.**

In this context of the popular use of drugs much of it is, of course, good. No doubt pharmacology has made tremendous contributions in curing diseases, lessening pain and extending our life spans. But much of it is not so good in that it can be a complete waste of money at least, and harmful or dangerous at worst.

Take vitamins. We spend billions each year obediently taking our multipurpose pills with perhaps one or two additional C's, D's or E's. We get psychological benefits in feeling that we've provided insurance that our bodies will get the nutrients the experts recommend. Yet nutritionists, doctors and other health professionals tell us that if we eat sensibly — a variety and enough of the right foods — we don't need vitamins. Well, in well-fed America where our problem is that we are overindulging at the dinner table, this may be the last country that needs vitamins. Better we should send them to the starving children of Africa or India. Having said that, you'll probably keep taking your one-a-day . . . and so will I.

Some of you may remember this. In the middle of the last century a clever and massive advertising campaign introduced a product called *Hadacol.* It was touted as a cure for a laundry list of infirmities and sicknesses. People literally (and remember I only use "literally," literally) stood in lines to buy the wonder elixir. "Testimonials" gave evidence of the power of the product and for months it was the #1 medicine (?) sold in the United States. It wasn't long before the medical profession debunked the extravagant claims and *Hadacol* quickly disappeared from shelves. Just before its demise, a reporter interviewed the man responsible for the product's extraordinary run. He asked: "What, if anything, is *Hadacol* really good for?" The entrepreneur replied candidly: "About a million bucks for me last year."

**Every prescription drug and most over-the-counter pills have possible side effects.**

Wasting money is one thing, but endangering life is another much more serious matter. Every prescription drug and most of the over-the-counter pills have a host of possible side effects ranging from simple headache, nausea or dizziness to convulsions, ulcers, blindness, heart arrest and — *the ultimate side effect* — death! Millions of Americans are abusing prescription drugs, according to Alan J. Leshner, head of the National Institute on Drug Abuse. NIDA also reported that in the period from 1990 to 1998, new users of pain relievers rose by 181 percent; new use of tranquilizers went up 132 percent and the use of stimulants climbed 165 percent. We *are* the other drug culture.

## Contextica and Terrorism

Dates are difficult to remember, but there are now two which are indelibly impressed on the memories of Americans. Pearl Harbor's December $7^{th}$, of course, and now 9/11 with its eerie coincidence of numerals to our emergency call numbers. Both dates will "live in infamy."

When those four jetliners were converted into deadly missiles killing almost 3,000 innocent people, utterly destroying the Twin Trade Towers and blowing away part of the country's military headquarters at the Pentagon, we were shocked into the realization that terrorism was not something that just happened in other countries but had, indeed, come home.

Suddenly the fear of traveling — or going anywhere for that matter — gripped the nation. Airline operations were suspended, but people were fearful about going anywhere which could be the next target. The Olympic Games, in the aftermath of 9/11, were the most heavily guarded of any such events in all of history. Sociologists were predicting the further cocooning of the family in which staying home (in the global or neighborhood sense) would be a dominant characteristic of the American culture for years to come. Terrorism will be with us, unfortunately, for the foreseeable future. Surely, in such times, it becomes critically important that we give a great deal of attention to the contexts in which we place ourselves.

**Scheduled air travel is six times safer than ground transportation.**

And yet, at the same time, a reality check may be in order. After 9/11, several of my acquaintances (some of yours too?) vowed never to put themselves into the context of an airliner again. That's lamentable and unwise because they'd be depriving themselves of (probably second only to walking) the safest way to travel. Studies based on hard statistics have consistently shown that scheduled air line travel is at least *six times safer* than journeying by automobile. Of course, when a plane crashes or is taken hostage, the entire world knows about it immediately. As you are reading these lines, however, hundreds of scheduled airplanes are carrying thousands of people, covering millions of miles without incident. Concurrently, 140 Americans will lose their lives today and every day of the year in vehicular traffic accidents. (That's an average drawn from an annual loss of 40,000 victims.) Except for the Labor and Memorial Day weekends, the media doesn't make much note of the *daily* carnage on the highways as it's not dramatic news.

But for my friends who are more influenced with the drama than the statistics, the anxiety persists. Franklin Delano Roosevelt's memorable words are relevant here. "The only thing we have to fear . . . is fear itself." We are social beings with a history of the need to travel, to migrate, to occasionally relocate in spite of any attendant dangers.

While some may be guilty of overreacting to that fateful September day, it would be foolish to ignore the potential dangers of the terrorist fanatics. We should certainly be cautiously aware of the times we are in and the contexts we choose. Statistics are alarming. In the decade of the 70s, the total number of confirmed terrorist incidents world-wide was 8,114. In the 1980s the figure skyrocketed to a grand total of 31,246. In the 90's there were over 56,000! The vast majority of acts of terrorism have (and still do) occur in *other* countries with the middle east, Europe, Africa and Latin America accounting for the largest percentages. The United States of America is still one of the safest of countries in which to travel. Indeed, blessed with our affluence and power, we've expended billions since 9/11 to further enhance an already high level of safety and security for domestic travel.

But, citizens journeying beyond our borders would be well-advised to pay greater attention to the contextica of their excursions. This is certainly not the *time* to visit *places* like the (now unholy) holy lands of the middle east.There are, also, other areas of the world where it's downright dangerous to be an American. As a matter of fact, our State Department has issued advisories to travelers in some countries to *disguise their nationalities* by not wearing identifying clothing or speaking Englsh in certain circles. Sad, but true. A lot of people hate us because we're so darned rich and powerful.

In early 2002, the State Department issued a warning to U.S. citizens in the Italian cities of Venice, Florence, Milan and Verona that there was a possible threat to Americans there from extremist groups.

Even in historic Vienna, the U.S. Embassy was closed in February, 2002, with a warning about a plot targeting 7,000 U.S. expatriates residing there. In the same month, the State Department ordered all nonessential staff and dependents to leave its embassy in Pakistan. There have been similar actions taken by our embassies in Bosnia, Peru and other locations.

Terrorist thugs regularly kidnap and sometimes murder tourists for ransom money in the Philippines and Columbia, with the latter holding the shameful record for the highest numbers of those incidents.

In Istanbul, Turkey, an American visitor from New Jersey was found in an alley a day after he was abducted from a shopping area where he was waiting for his wife. The frantic woman had immediately reported his disappearance to the police who suggested she return to the area the next morning. She did so and there was her husband lying in a semi-stupor minus his wallet . . . and one kidney! Apparently the organ theft was not an unheard of occurrence as the police surmised what had happened. A frightening thought: perhaps *they* were in on it. The relatively stable central American country of Costa Rica has had problems. When I visited there in 1999, an American was robbed after having his throat slashed. He survived but, understandably, vowed never to return.

Faced with the reality of potential violence in just about any corner of the world, what is one to do? Stay within the much safer borders of the U.S.A? The contextica *is* much more favorable here in our own back yard. But the allures of seeing the Taj Mahal, the pyramids, the Great Wall, the barrier reef, the Acropolis, the rain forests, the deserts, the mountains or skiing the Alps, riding in a safari, observing other cultures or visiting our roots are very enticing. Besides, we are not going to give in to the terrorists.

If travel we must — and we must — the creative contexter can get valuable guidance from two major sources. The State Department puts out its *Public Announcements* which has the most up-to-date information about terrorist threats and other conditions that may pose problems for traveling Americans. Beyond that, they also publish *Consular Information* sheets for every country in the world. Those include information about: crime, health conditions, entry requirements, areas of instability and the locations of the nearest embassy or consulate in that particular country.

A good travel agent should also be able to apprise you of that same intelligence. They may, in addition, know the reactions of clients who have just returned from the particular destinations in which you are interested. Benefit from their experiences; glean all the knowledge you can. Just as you wouldn't start a long automobile trip without checking the gas tank, you shouldn't embark on an odyssey without all the information you can get relating to a safe contextica. You don't want to be in the wrong place at the wrong time.

## The Best of Times, The Worst of Times

As we have entered the new millennium there is plenty of evidence to support pessimism. Drug abuse is rampant; crime is a national problem with prisons much overcrowded; divorces about equal marriages; too many children are born to unmarried teenage mothers; politicians put their tenure above their constituents' good; the stress of making ends meet takes its toll in the curses of ulcers, heart failure, neuroses and psychoses; the threats of nuclear holocaust and fanatical terrorism in the forms of suicidal destruction and biochemical warfare are constantly with us as nations and cultures continue to square off against each other. As automation and robotics increase along with the emerging industrialization of the Orient, many will lose their jobs. Incurable diseases such as AIDS annihilate millions and unfed children in third world countries die slow, horrible deaths.

Much of our behavior is described as — if not immoral — amoral. In these contexts the words of Shakespeare easily come to mind when he lamented: "How weary, stale, flat and improfitable seem to me all the uses of this world."

The human spirit, however, has proved itself to be indomitable throughout history. Bubonic plagues and potato famines have been survived, all wars have ended in relative peace, cool heads have prevailed so that humankind has not been obliterated even after the discoveries of gunpowder, poison gases or nuclear bombs. Medical science has cured many diseases and enabled us to live

**The human spirit has proved itself to be indomitable throughout history.**

much longer, fuller lives. Advances in technology allow instant communication with anyone and new modes of travel take us swiftly to any place on earth . . . and beyond.

Certainly a much stronger case can be made for choosing optimism over pessimism. We are the most advantaged of all who have ever lived in the history of humankind. Just sixty years ago, the richest people didn't have the material goods, the health and medicine, the opportunities and the privileges that the average citizen in America has today. Creative thinking has solved the challenges of the past and will (with *your* help) continue to foster civilization's continuing progress. Now, more than ever, we have the options of leading richer, fuller and more productive lives by creatively contexting ourselves so as to ensure that we will enjoy the very best of times.

## Finally

Thanks for taking your very valuable time (*all time is valuable*) to let me share my thoughts with you. It's been said that if after attending a lecture, taking a course, participating in a workshop or reading a book, you can come away with just *one* provocative thought or idea, it will have been worthwhile. It is my sincere hope that *isn't* the case here. No, I would hope that there would have been at least two or three ideas — or more — from these pages. One of those could be that you would want to continue your journey into the fascinating realm of creative thinking. I've only touched upon many areas in an effort to be comprehensive, but I recognize that some depth has been sacrificed. Please, then, make use of the references listed to continue your further exploration. If this book has served a seminal function in encouraging your interest, I'll be elated knowing that a very important contribution may have been made. Developing your individual situational savvy in a highly complex society is a very personal activity and no one book can possibly give final answers to anyone. At least, maybe a start and a good road map have been provided.

Every now and then, ask yourself: ***where am I and, what time is it ?*** Please get into the habit of applying creative thinking to your life's problems. The skills, techniques, and concepts presented will, of course, take time to integrate into your daily life. They're of little value without taking action, and remember, you must be your own motivator. But please don't wait. *There really is only one time* **. . .** ***Now!***

**A final nudge . . . Don't let this happen to you!**

**Godspeed . . .**

***wind at your back . . .***

***have a great creatively-contexted life!***

# REFERENCES


Barnett, Jo Ellen, *Time's Pendulum*, NYC: Plenum Publishing Corporation, 1998.

Csikszentmihalyi, Mihaly, *Creativity,* NYC: Harper Collins, 1996.

Cousins, Norman, *Human Options*, NYC: Berkely Publishing Company, 1981.

Devine, William F. *Women, Men and Money*, NYC: Crown Publishing, 1998.

Gates, Bill, *Business at the Speed of Thought, NYC*: Warner Books, 1999.

Glasser, William, *Taking Effective Control of Your Life*, NYC: Harper & Row, 1984.

Glass, Lillian, *Attracting Terrific People*, NYC: Scribner, 1997.

*Happiness Explained,* U.S. News & World Report, September 3, 2001.

Joseph, Lawrence E. *Common Sense*, NYC: Addison-Wesley Publishing, 1994.

Khalsa, Dharma, *Brain Longevity*, NYC: Warner Books, 1997.

LeDoux, *The Synaptic Self,* NYC: Viking, 2002.

Manning, Richard F. *Developing Creative Thinking in Teachers and Students,* Research Project Report # 45-74-524-1, U.S. Office Of Education, Washington, D.C., 1976.

Manning, Richard F. *The Classroom of the Future,* Ohio Schools, Columbus, OH: September, 1967.

Manning, Richard F. *Mobility and Leadership,* Cleveland, Ohio: Case Western Reserve University Press, 1968.

Norman, R. *Augustine's Travels*, NYC: American Mangement Association, 1997.

Norville, Deborah, *Back on Track*, NYC: Simon & Schuster, 1997.

Osborne, Alex. *Applied Imagination*, 3rd edition. NYC: Scribner, 1963.

Parnes, Sidney, *Creativity: Unlocking Human Potential,* Buffalo, NYC: D.O.K. Pub., 1972.

Pynchon, John, *Terrorism, NYC:* Kensington Publishing Company, 2002.

Raines, Robert, *A Time to Live*, NYC: Penquin Books, 1997.

Sagan, Carl, *Billions and Billions*, NYC: Random House, 1997.

Spezzzano, Charles, *What to Do between Life and Death*, NYC:Wm. Morrow and Company, 1992.

Taylor, Calvin W. (Ed.) *Climate for Creativity.* Elmsford, NYC: Pergammon, 1971.

Taylor, Jack W. *How to Create New Ideas,* Englewood Cliffs, NJ: Prentice-Hall, 1961.

Torrance, E.P. *Guiding Creative Talent,* Englewood Cliffs, N.J: Prentice-Hall, 1962.